lease remember that this is a library book, and that it belongs only temporarily to each person who uses it. Be considerate. Do not write in this, or any, library book.

P9-DFV-425

THE FIRST-YEAR EXPERIENCE
MONOGRAPH SERIES No. **30**

Professing the Disciplines

An Analysis of Senior Seminars and Capstone Courses

WITHDRAWN

Jean M. Henscheid

With
John E. Breitmeyer
and
Jessica L. Mercer

**National Resource Center for The First-Year Experience® and Students in Transition
University of South Carolina, 2000**

Cite as:

Henscheid, J. M. (2000). *Professing the disciplines: An analysis of senior seminars and capstone courses* (Monograph No. 30). Columbia, SC: University of South Carolina, National Resource Center for The First-Year Experience and Students in Transition.

Additional copies of this monograph may be ordered at $30 each from the National Resource Center for The First-Year Experience and Students in Transition, University of South Carolina, 1629 Pendleton Street, Columbia, SC 29208. Telephone (803) 777-6029. Telefax (803) 777-4699.

Copyright 2000, by the University of South Carolina. All rights reserved.
No part of this work may be reproduced or copied in any form, by any means,
without written permission of the University of South Carolina.

ISBN Number: 1-889271-32-2

The Freshman Year Experience® and The First-Year Experience® are trademarks of the University of South Carolina. A license may be granted upon written request to use the terms "The Freshman Year Experience" and "The First-Year Experience." This license is not transferrable without written approval of the University of South Carolina.

Acknowledgments

The author thanks the following individuals for their contributions to this monograph:

John N. Gardner, senior fellow of the National Resource Center for The First-Year Experience and Students in Transition, who called for this study, and Betsy Barefoot, co-director of The Policy Center on The First Year of College, who, along with Carrie Warnock of the National Resource Center, administered the survey. Thank you to John, Betsy, and Stuart Hunter, director of the National Resource Center, for their comments on initial drafts. Thank you to the National Resource Center's Vicky Howell for entering the survey data.

Jessica Mercer and John Breitmeyer, who were instrumental in the analyses of these data, as were John Lane and Philip Moore, all of the University of South Carolina.

The National Resource Center's Katrina Chandler and Tracy Skipper, who were responsible for the layout and design of this publication, and Scott Slawinski who contributed to the design, proof read the chapters, and significantly improved the clarity of the writing.

Contents

Chapter 1

The Senior Year Experience and Senior Curriculum

Chapter 2

WITHDRAWN

Survey Results for All Senior Seminars and Capstone Courses

Methodology, Aggregate Results by

Chapter 3

Survey Results for Discipline- and Department-based Courses

Results by Institution Type,

Chapter 3

Chapter 4

Chapter 5

Chapter 6

Summary of Analysis and Conclusions

Appendix A

Examples of Courses

Appendix B

Survey Instrument

Appendix C

Responding Institutions

Chapter 1

The Senior-Year Experience and Senior Curriculum

Introduction

This monograph is about senior seminars and capstone courses offered at American colleges and universities. It reports on data collected during the summer of 1999 on 864 courses offered at institutions throughout the country to the smallest, most persistent undergraduate cohort – college and university seniors.

Increasing the number of American students who achieve a place in this cohort was, at the time of this writing, central campaign rhetoric for presidential candidates Al Gore and George W. Bush. Co-opting the sentiment of the Children's Defense Fund, these and other candidates, the American public, and the media were focused on discovering strategies for ensuring that no child would be left behind by the education establishment.

In terms of high school completion and college degree attainment, the facts at the time of this campaign were that many American children had little chance of becoming college seniors and were being left far behind. Although overall education levels were climbing, some 30% of American students were still not graduating from high school. Of those who finished and started college as full-time students, only half would receive their bachelor's degrees within five years. Fewer than 10% of students who enrolled initially at two-year institutions would complete bachelor's degrees in five years. The picture improved for students at higher socioeconomic levels and among those with parents who had attained higher levels of formal education (National Center for Education Statistics, 2000).

The overall result was, and is, that by the time American students become college seniors, they have withstood an educational filter that sifts out up to 70% of their peers. Some students who do not achieve a straight trajectory from first grade to college graduation may return to finish years later. Many will not. Those students who do complete college will, over their life times, earn the highest salaries, be the least dependent on public financial assistance, pay the most in taxes, contribute the most to charities, commit the fewest crimes, and make the best consumer decisions (The Institute for Higher Education Policy, 1998). Given this potential and their resilience, college seniors, as a group, may be viewed as among America's most successful students. Likewise, what seniors are taught may be considered an important indicator of what educators want students to retain from their years in higher education and what they want these students to be and do in the future. The survey reported in this monograph was conducted to look inside those courses that serve as the college synthesis and send-off, where American colleges and universities may be collectively telling their students, it all comes down to this...

This report is further offered to help illuminate the national discussion around two questions: What and how should America teach all of its college students? Both questions have been thoroughly and increasingly considered over the past decade at conferences and in journals such as *College Teaching, Daedalus, The Journal of General Education, The Journal of the First-Year Experience and Students in Transition,* and *Pedagogy Journal;* in periodicals including *Change, About Campus,* and *The Chronicle of Higher Education;* in books such as *Scholarship Reconsidered* (Boyer, 1990), *Classroom Research* (Cross & Steadman, 1998), *Scholarship Assessed* (Glassick, Huber, & Maeroff, 1996), and *Undergraduate Education* (Weingartner, 1992); and in all of the volumes of the Jossey-Bass *New Directions for Teaching and Learning* series. The intent is to provide evidentiary food for thought to educators involved in this, a dialogue recently characterized by Hutchings and Shulman (1999) as stepping back, or "going meta," to systematically examine questions related to student learning (p. 13).

Past Reviews of Senior Seminars and Capstone Courses

Preceding the survey reported in this monograph, three efforts have been made to count and catalog the characteristics of modern senior seminars and capstone courses. In the 1970s, the Carnegie Council on Policy Studies in Higher Education sponsored a study of a representative sample of 270 college and university catalogs for 1975. Among its other purposes, this study served to list the number of instances of senior seminars connected with general education programs. That count revealed that, at the time, only 3% of institutions sponsored senior seminars "designed to cap the general education experience by application of different student majors to a common problem" (Levine, p. 19). These courses were more prevalent in arts and sciences colleges (4%), than in professional or technical colleges (1%). Arthur Levine, who reported this study in his *Handbook of Undergraduate Education* (1978), noted later (1998) that senior seminars and capstone courses (a term used interchangeably throughout the literature) have appeared, disappeared, and reappeared throughout the history of American higher education and have historically been offered by 1 in 20 institutions nationwide.

Joseph Cuseo (1998) conducted a second study of these courses by reviewing proceedings from four national Conferences on The Senior Year Experience and two national Conferences on Students in Transition—all forums established to discuss the senior year experience sponsored by the National Resource Center for The First-Year Experience and Students in Transition. His analysis did not attempt to count the number of institutions offering senior seminars or capstone courses; rather, it attempted to characterize and categorize the goals that undergird senior year experience programs, including credit-bearing courses. Cuseo found that three overarching purposes of what is termed the Senior Year Experience Movement were evidenced in the proceedings and included: (a) bringing integration and closure to the undergraduate experience, (b) providing students with an opportunity to reflect on the meaning of their college experience, and (c) facilitating graduating students' transition to postcollege life. According to these conference presentations, the varying aspects of the senior year experience, including senior seminars and capstone courses are intended to:

- Promote the coherence and relevance of general education
- Promote integration and connections between general education and the academic major
- Foster integration and synthesis within the academic major
- Promote meaningful connections between the academic major and work (career) experiences
- Explicitly and intentionally develop important student skills, competencies, and perspectives that are tacitly or incidentally developed in the college curriculum (for example, leadership skills and character and values development)

♦ Enhance awareness of and support for the key personal adjustments encountered by seniors during their transition from college to post college life

♦ Improve seniors' career preparation and pre-professional development, that is, facilitate their transition from the academic to the professional world

♦ Enhance seniors' preparation and prospects for postgraduate education

♦ Promote effective life planning and decision making with respect to practical issues likely to be encountered in adult life after college (for example, financial planning, marriage, and family planning)

♦ Encourage a sense of unity and community among the senior class, which can serve as a foundation for later alumni networking and future alumni support of the college. (Cuseo, 1998, p. 22)

In the report of his review, Cuseo (1998) notes that the senior year capstone course, as described by these conference participants, has been used as a "major vehicle" to bring coherence and closure to the general education experience. It does so by forging "interdisciplinary connections among the liberal arts and sciences" (p. 23). Cuseo further reports that capstone courses and senior seminars have been designed and offered by institutions across the country to achieve all but the last of the 10 goals he identified, that last being to encourage a sense of unity and community among the senior class. This goal, Cuseo notes, may be seen as both a purpose and a byproduct of these programs and courses.

A follow-up review of proceedings from four additional Students in Transition Conferences (which, by this time, had subsumed the Senior Year Experience meetings) held between 1997 and 1999 revealed a continued interest in all 10 of the goals listed above. This review, conducted by Scott Slawinski, editorial assistant at the National Resource Center for The First-Year Experience and Students in Transition, suggested that educators who attend these conferences were primarily interested in discussing methods employed on their campuses to prepare seniors for their careers and to promote an integration between general education and the academic major.

The third and final review of modern senior seminars and capstone courses was conducted by the author in August 2000 on abstracts of presentations delivered on and articles written about these courses and available through the Educational Resources Information Center (ERIC) database (http://ericir.syr.edu/Eric/). These abstracts written during or after 1990 suggest that these courses are almost universally affiliated with an academic discipline. Among 14 abstracts of presentations and publications generated by a search of the ERIC database on the keywords "senior capstone," three of the courses described were offered through collaboration between departments or through a central academic unit, such as the office of the chief academic officer. The other 11 were discipline specific with the largest number of the courses offered through speech, communications, and/or theatre departments. The primary goal of these courses is almost exclusively to foster integration and synthesis within the academic major. The second most frequently cited primary goal, much lower on the list, is to improve the students' career preparation and pre-professional development. Just one course is described as promoting integration and connections between general education and the academic major. Course descriptions for and research results on both senior seminars and capstone courses with few exceptions were reported to discipline-specific audiences, across a wide spectrum of disciplines.

Among these abstracts on senior seminars written between 1990 and August 2000, all but two were single discipline offerings. In nine, the primary goal is described as promoting integration and synthesis within the major, with the next highest goal again being the improvement of students' career preparation and pre-professional development. Abstracts pulled from both searches on capstone courses and senior seminars indicate that the courses are intended to cement the student's disciplinary affiliation, to provide a rite of passage into the world of work or graduate school as a member of a distinct scholarly community, and to integrate the skills and knowledge acquired in the discipline. No discernable differences exist between the descriptions of senior seminars and senior capstone courses, and in several instances, the two searches generated the same abstracts.

The predilection toward a single disciplinary focus during the senior year revealed in this small sample of ERIC abstracts may be an artifact of the necessity felt by most academic faculty members to share their pedagogical approaches and research findings through publications and presentations, a necessity not as strongly felt by other members of the academy who may also offer these senior level courses. Or it may expose a true predominance of the disciplines. What it does is both corroborate and contradict the reviews conducted by Levine, Cuseo, and Slawinski and offer support for necessity of the study reported here.

What Colleges Teach Seniors

The title of this monograph, *Professing the Disciplines*, foreshadows the major finding of this survey that senior seminars and capstone courses across all types of American colleges and universities are generally designed to leave students with an understanding of and appreciation for single academic disciplines. Results of this First National Survey of Senior Seminars and Capstone Courses confirm Levine's findings and the ERIC database searches, reorder Cuseo and Slawinski's lists, and in the aggregate, build a picture of these courses generally focused on specialization and preparation for work in the field of the academic major. Survey findings also indicate that:

- ◆ The least likely instructional components to be found in senior seminars and capstone courses are those that take students out of the classroom, either into the work place, into the community, or as part of an educational travel experience.

- ◆ Senior seminars and capstone courses are most often taught by faculty members working alone and most courses, including interdisciplinary courses, are administered by single academic departments.

- ◆ Most senior seminars and capstone courses are not part of a comprehensive assessment process. When they are evaluated, it is by the students and faculty members who participate in these courses.

This First National Survey on Senior Seminars and Capstone Courses indicates that through these courses, colleges teach seniors how to be members of their disciplinary communities. According to these results, individual academic faculty members in these small courses tie up the loose ends of learning in the major and presage the world of work in the field or fields represented by that major. This survey indicates that the culminating academic experience at America's colleges and universities most frequently caps not the whole of college, but a specialized piece of that experience.

Intended Monograph Audience

The survey and this report were conceived as the result of a promise made by John Gardner and Gretchen Van der Veer in their 1998 book, *The Senior Year Experience*—that the National Resource Center on The First-Year Experience and Students in Transition would expand the literature base on college seniors. At that time, Gardner and Van der Veer reported that one aspect of the senior year experience, the senior seminar or capstone course, was particularly in need of study. This monograph was written primarily for educators interested in improving the academic experience of students nearing the end of their college career. As with much of the work sponsored through the National Resource Center for The First-Year Experience and Students in Transition, the readership of this monograph is potentially diverse; it just as easily could include curriculum designers and administrators, as it could classroom faculty, educational researchers, and other educators.

Methods, Display of Results, and Analyses

Some 4,285 surveys were sent to chief academic and student affairs officers and career services directors at 1,683 regionally accredited institutions with upper division students. The surveys were mailed during the first week of May in 1999 and respondents were given four months to complete and return them to the National Resource Center. The decision was made to discard some 20 surveys on which respondents from one part of an institution indicated that their college or university did not sponsor a senior seminar or capstone course while another respondent from another part of the same institution indicated that such a course existed.

In total, 707 institutions responded to the survey, including 256 public and 451 private, for a response rate of 42%. The survey instruments were designed to allow the forms to be duplicated and distributed by the original survey recipients, which resulted in 404 responses being returned from institutions sending in more than one survey. In total, 549 institutions (77.6%) of the 707 that responded indicated that they offered at least one senior seminar or capstone course.

A total of 1,028 surveys were returned from these 707 institutions. In all, 164 respondents indicated that their institutions did not currently offer senior capstones or senior seminars. The results of this survey, then, are based upon descriptions of 864 courses. Respondents who indicated that their institutions did offer seniors seminars and/or capstone courses were asked to select and report on just one of four course types, including discipline- or department-based courses, interdisciplinary courses, transition courses, or career planning courses. Forty respondents selected "other" to describe their course type.

The survey data reported here were collected to identify and compare senior seminars and capstone courses across American colleges and universities. Key variables in this research are (a) type of institution (public or private), (b) level of institutional enrollment (under 1,000; 1001 to 5,000; 5,001 to 10,000; or over 10,000 students), and (c) institutional selectivity (high, medium, and low). This selectivity level was self-reported by the respondents.

Survey findings are displayed from the greatest to smallest number of courses reported on in the survey, beginning with aggregate results and analyses in Chapter 2. The findings and analysis on discipline- and department-based courses, by far the largest number of courses described by respondents, are displayed in Chapter 3; interdisciplinary courses are described and analyzed in Chapter 4; and the three smallest groups of courses are listed in Chapter 5. These final three course types include transition courses, career planning courses, and "other" courses which respondents indicated did not fit into any of the categories listed on the survey instrument. "Other" courses were listed by respondents as research and senior thesis projects, internships, service-learning opportunities, senior integrative experiences, and special topics courses. Just over a combined total of 100 respondents completed surveys on courses falling into the final three course types. Because statistical analyses on such a small number of responses would be suspect, a decision was made to summarize these findings in narrative.

In all cases chi-square analyses were performed to determine the significance of differences. Summaries of findings of potentially greatest interest are offered in single columns beside the tables and a summary of analysis is offered at the end of each of the next three chapters. Chapter 3 also displays data by disciplinary cluster as they were selected and collapsed from the categories devised by the American Council on Education (Anderson, 1998).

Chapters 2 through 5 each offer analyses of 11 components of senior seminars and capstone courses by the key variables. These 11 components include:

- Goals of the course – Each respondent was asked to choose all goals that directly applied to the course they were describing from a list of nine goals mirroring those for senior seminars and capstones courses originated by Cuseo (1998) as noted above. Rather than attempt to compare all course goals selected by respondents, a decision was made to compare only those goals marked by respondents with a "1." All course goal tables, then, compare only the primary goals of the courses, as reported by the respondents. A possible limitation of the Cuseo goal taxonomy and the survey instrument is the wording of the eighth goal, listed on the instrument as "enhancing seniors' preparation and prospects for postgraduate education." Few respondents selected this item, which may be attributable to confusion between post-undergraduate or graduate education and postgraduate education. Caution should therefore be exercised when generalizing from findings on this goal.

- Instructional responsibility – Each respondent was asked to indicate the type of staff member who teaches the course. Each respondent was asked to mark any of five options that apply to the course and was given the option to indicate whether the course is team taught or taught by one individual.

- Maximum section size of the course

- Amount and type of academic credit and grading practices – Each respondent was asked to indicate if the course is graded pass/fail, whether academic credit is granted, and, if so, how much credit is granted, and what type of credit is assigned to the course.

- Unit administering the course

- Instructional components – Each respondent was asked to select all of 15 possible instructional components used in the course they were describing.

- Populations required to take the course – Each respondent was asked to mark if all, some, or no students are required to take the course. Respondents also were asked to indicate the gender ratio of their course, if offered as an elective.

- Length of existence of the course at the institution

- Evaluation and assessment practices – Each respondent was asked to describe who evaluates the course and whether the course is tied to comprehensive institutional assessment.

The display of findings and analyses for each of the five types of courses is followed in Chapter 6 by a summary of all analyses, conclusions, and recommendations for future research. Appendix A provides examples of each course type. The survey instrument is included as Appendix B, and Appendix C provides a list of responding institutions by course type.

References

Anderson, C. J. (1998). *Fact book on higher education: 1997 edition.* Phoenix: American Council on Education and Oryx.

Boyer, E. L. (1990). *Scholarship reconsidered: Priorities of the professorate.* Princeton, NJ: Carnegie Foundation for the Advancement of Teaching.

The Chronicle of Higher Education Almanac. (1999, August 27), 7.

Cross, K. P., & Steadman, M. H. *(1996). Classroom research : Implementing the scholarship of teaching.* San Francisco: Jossey-Bass.

Cuseo, J. B. (1998). *Objectives and benefits of senior year programs.* In J. N. Gardner, Gretchen Van der Veer & Associates, *The senior year experience: Facilitating integration, reflection, closure, and transition* (pp. 21–36). San Francisco: Jossey-Bass.

Gardner, J. N., Van der Veer, G., & Associates. (1998). *The senior year experience: Facilitating integration, reflection, closure, and transition.* San Francisco: Jossey-Bass.

Glassick, C. E., Huber, M. T., & Maeroff, G. I. (1997). *Scholarship Assessed: Evaluation of the professorate.* San Francisco: Jossey-Bass.

Hutchings, P., & Shulman, L. S. (1999, September/October). *The scholarship of teaching. New elaborations, new developments. Change,* 11–15.

The Institute for Higher Education Policy. (1998). *Reaping the benefits: Defining the public and private value of going to college: The new millennium project on higher education costs, pricing, and productivity.* Washington, DC: Author. (ERIC Document Reproduction Service No. ED 420 256).

Levine, A. (1998). A president's personal and historical perspective. In J. N. Gardner, Gretchen Van der Veer & Associates, *The senior year experience: Facilitating integration, reflection, closure, and transition* (pp. 51–58). San Francisco: Jossey-Bass.

Levine, A. (1978). *Handbook of undergraduate curriculum.* San Francisco: Jossey-Bass.

National Center for Education Statistics (2000, August 26). *NCES fast facts.* Washington DC: Author. Retrieved August 26, 2000 from the World Wide Web: http://nces.ed.gov/fastfacts/display.asp?id=27

Pascarella, E. T., & Terenzini, P. T. (1991). *How college affects students: Findings and insights from 20 years of research.* San Francisco: Jossey-Bass.

Weingartner, R. H. (1992). *Undergraduate education: Goals and means.* New York: American Council on Education/Macmillan.

Chapter 2

Survey Results for All Senior Seminars and Capstone Courses

In this chapter, aggregate results are displayed for all 864 courses reported on by survey respondents. Tables 2.1 through 2.4 offer aggregate totals and percentages of responses by the three key variables, institution type, institution enrollment level, and institution selectivity. The chapter concludes with an aggregate summary of analysis for all senior seminars and capstone courses described by survey respondents.

Table 2.1
Total Number of Courses by Course Type (N = 864)

Course Type	Number	Percentage
Interdisciplinary capstone course	141	16.3%
Discipline or department-based course	607	70.3%
Career planning course	26	3.0%
Transition course (focusing on preparation for work, graduate school, life choice, life skills, or life after college)	50	5.8%
Other	40	4.6%

Note Multiple responses were received from individual institutions.

"Results of this survey suggest that…college and university seniors who enroll in senior seminars and capstone courses are most likely to engage in a culmination of learning in their academic major."

Table 2.2
Total Number of Courses by Institution Type (N = 864)

	Institution Type	
	Public	Private
Number	361	503
Percentage	41.7%	58.2%

Note. Multiple responses were received from individual institutions.

Table 2.3
Total Number of Courses by Enrollment Level (N = 864)

	Enrollment Level			
	1,000 and Under	1,001-5,000	5,001-10,000	Over 10,000
Number	176	387	112	189
Percentage	20.3%	44.7%	12.9%	21.8%

Note. Multiple responses were received from individual institutions.

Table 2.4
Total Number of Courses by Selectivity (N = 864)

	Selectivity		
	High	Medium	Low
Number	81	670	113
Percentage	9.3%	77.5%	13.0%

Note. Multiple responses were received from individual institutions.

Table 2.5
Number One Goal of Senior Seminars and Capstone Courses – All Courses (N = 864)

Goal	Rank Order
Fostering integration and synthesis within the academic major	1 (*n* = 440)
Promoting integration and connections between the academic major and work world	2 (*n* = 112)
Improving seniors' career preparation and pre-professional development	3 (*n* = 79)
Promoting integration and connections between general education and the academic major	4 (*n* = 50)
Promoting the coherence and relevance of general education	5 (*n* = 44)
Explicitly and intentionally developing important student skills, competencies, and perspectives which are tacitly or incidentally developed in the college curriculum (e.g., leadership skills)	5 (*n* = 44)
Other	6 (*n* = 29)
Promoting effective life planning and decision making with respect to issues that will be encountered in adult life after college	7 (*n* – 23)
Enhancing seniors' preparation and prospects for postgraduate education	8 (*n* = 21)
Enhancing awareness of and support for key personal adjustments encountered by seniors during their transition from college to post-college life	9 (*n* = 17)

Note. Totals do not add to 100%. Some respondents selected more than one primary goal.

1. Course Goals

According to the results of this survey, senior seminars and capstone courses are overwhelmingly intended to cap learning within the academic major (Table 2.5 through 2.8). When examined together (Table 2.5) the courses described by respondents are nearly four times more likely to focus on the academic major than they are to attend to connecting the academic major to the work world, the second most frequently cited number one goal. However, the second and third most frequently marked number one goals both concern the work world.

"...the second and third most frequently marked number one goals both concern the work world."

Much lower on the list, linking general education with the academic major was listed by only 50 respondents as primarily important in the courses they described. Goals outside the academic major and the work world, including life planning, preparing for postgraduate education, and personal development, trailed in importance. According to these respondents, public and private institutions share similar goals for these senior seminars and capstone courses (Table 2.6).

Table 2.6

Number One Goal of Senior Seminars and Capstone Courses – All Courses by Institution Type (N = 864)

Goal	Public (N = 361)	Private (N = 503)
	Institution Type	
Fostering integration and synthesis within the academic major	1 (n = 192)	1 (n = 248)
Promoting integration and connections between the academic major and work world	2 (n = 59)*	2 (n = 53)
Improving seniors' career preparation and pre-professional development	3 (n = 37)	3 (n = 42)
Promoting integration and connections between general education and the academic major	5 (n = 13)*	4 (n = 37)
Promoting the coherence and relevance of general education	4 (n = 18)	6 (n = 26)
Explicitly and intentionally developing important student skills, competencies, and perspectives which are tacitly or incidentally developed in the college curriculum (e.g., leadership skills)	5 (n = 13)	5 (n = 31)
Other	8 (n = 6)*	7 (n = 23)
Promoting effective life planning and decision making with respect to issues that will be encountered in adult life after college	9 (n = 5)*	8 (n = 18)
Enhancing seniors' preparation and prospects for postgraduate education	7 (n = 8)	9 (n = 13)
Enhancing awareness of and support for key personal adjustments encountered by seniors during their transition from college to post-college life	6 (n = 9)	10 (n = 8)

Note. Totals do not add to 100%. Some respondents selected more than one primary goal.

*p<.05

"...linking general education with the academic major was listed by only 30 respondents as primarily important..."

Table 2.7

Number One Goal of Senior Seminars and Capstone Courses – All Courses by Institution Enrollment Level (N = 864)

Goal	Enrollment Level			
	1,000 and Under	1,001-5,000	5,001-10,000	Over 10,000
Fostering integration and synthesis within the academic major	1 (n = 74)*	1 (n = 210)	1 (n = 64)	1 (n = 92)
Promoting integration and connections between the academic major and work world	2 (n = 20)	2 (n = 50)	2 (n = 12)	2 (n = 30)
Improving seniors' career preparation and pre-professional development	2 (n = 20)	3 (n = 28)	4 (n = 8)	3 (n = 23)
Promoting integration and connections between general education and the academic major	3 (n = 16)	4 (n = 20)	6 (n = 6)	6 (n = 8)
Promoting the coherence and relevance of general education	4 (n = 14)*	8 (n = 11)	3 (n = 10)	5 (n = 9)
Explicitly and intentionally developing important student skills, competencies, and perspectives which are tacitly or incidentally developed in the college curriculum (e.g., leadership skills)	5 (n = 10)	5 (n = 17)	5 (n = 7)	4 (n = 10)
Other	6 (n = 8)*	6 (n = 16)	10 (n = 1)	7 (n = 4)
Promoting effective life planning and decision making with respect to issues that will be encountered in adult life after college	8 (n = 6)	7 (n = 13)	9 (n = 2)	8 (n = 2)
Enhancing seniors' preparation and prospects for postgraduate education	7 (n = 7)	9 (n = 8)	7 (n = 4)	8 (n = 2)
Enhancing awareness of and support for key personal adjustments encountered by seniors during their transition from college to post-college life	9 (n =5)	10 (n = 5)	8 (n = 3)	7 (n = 4)

Note. Totals do not add to 100%. Some respondents selected more than one primary goal.

*p<.05

Respondents from institutions with enrollments of 1,001 to 5,000 students notably were less likely to mark promoting the coherence and relevance of general education as a number one goal for the courses they were describing than were other respondents (Table 2.7). General education appears eighth on a list of ten possible number one goals.

"General education appears eighth on a list of ten possible number one goals."

Respondents from institutions of medium selectivity were also less likely to single out general education as primarily important, particularly as compared to highly selective institutions (Table 2.8). Care should be taken when generalizing from these findings, as the number of responses to this question was small from institutions of high and low selectivity. The same caveat applies in all instances where the number of responses is small.

Table 2.8

Number One Goal of Senior Seminars and Capstone Courses – All Courses by Institution Selectivity (N = 864)

	Selectivity		
Goal	High (*n* = 81)	Medium (*n* = 670)	Low (*n* = 113)
Fostering integration and synthesis within the academic major	1 (*n* = 49)	1 (*n* = 339)	1 (*n* = 52)
Promoting integration and connections between the academic major and work world	4 (*n* = 3)*	2 (*n* = 89)	2 (*n* = 20)
Improving seniors' career preparation and pre-professional development	3 (*n* = 4)	3 (*n* = 65)	3 (*n* = 10)
Promoting integration and connections between general education and the academic major	5 (*n* = 2)	4 (*n* = 41)	4 (*n* = 7)
Promoting the coherence and relevance of general education	2 (*n* = 5)	6 (*n* = 34)	5 (*n* = 5)
Explicitly and intentionally developing important student skills, competencies, and perspectives which are tacitly or incidentally developed in the college curriculum (e.g., leadership skills)	5 (*n* = 2)	5 (*n* = 35)	4 (*n* = 7)
Other	2 (*n* = 5)	7 (*n* = 22)	6 (*n* = 2)
Promoting effective life planning and decision making with respect to issues that will be encountered in adult life after college	6 (*n* = 1)	8 (*n* = 20)	6 (*n* = 2)
Enhancing seniors' preparation and prospects for postgraduate education	6 (*n* = 1)*	9 (*n* = 19)	7 (*n* = 1)
Enhancing awareness of and support for key personal adjustments encountered by seniors during their transition from college to post-college life	6 (*n* = 1)	10 (*n* = 14)	6 (*n* = 2)

Note. Totals do not add to 100%. Some respondents selected more than one primary goal.

*$p<.05$

Table 2.9
Instructional Responsibility for Senior Seminars and Capstone Courses – All Courses (N = 864)

Instructional staff	Exclusive Responsibility	As Part of a Team
Faculty	$n = 565$	$n = 245$
Career professionals	$n = 37$	$n = 24$
Community leaders	$n = 21$	$n = 32$
Other	$n = 9$	$n = 7$
Other student affairs professionals	$n = 7$	$n = 6$
Graduate students	$n = 3$	$n = 2$

Note. Totals do not add to 100%. Some sections of the same course are taught by different individuals.

2. Instructional Responsibility

This survey indicates that, overwhelmingly, academic faculty members are responsible for teaching senior seminars and capstone courses, as lone instructors or as members of instructional teams (Table 2.9). Only three graduate students were reported to have exclusive responsibility for these courses and only two respondents reported that graduate students teach these courses in concert with others or that they would be selected from a list of choices. The respondents indicated that student affairs professionals not connected with career service centers are only slightly more likely to teach courses described in this survey, either exclusively or as part of a team, than graduate students. The survey indicated that a far greater number of community leaders are asked to teach these courses, alone or as part of an instructional team, than non-career center student affairs professionals.

"...overwhelmingly, academic faculty members are responsible for teaching senior seminars and capstone courses..."

Community leaders are more likely to be asked to serve as members of teaching teams, both at public and private institutions (Table 2.10), than they are to teach alone. This holds true at institutions with enrollments of between 1,001 and 5,000 and those over 10,000 (Table 2.11).

Table 2.10
Instructional Responsibility for Senior Seminars and Capstone Courses – All Courses by Institution Type   (N = 864)

| | Exclusive Responsibility | | As Part of a Team | |
Instructional staff	Public	Private	Public	Private
Faculty	$n = 252$	$n = 313$	$n = 88$	$n = 157$
Career professionals	$n = 12^*$	$n = 25$	$n = 10$	$n = 14$
Community leaders	$n = 9^{**}$	$n = 12^{**}$	$n = 11$	$n = 21$
Other	$n = 4$	$n = 5$	$n = 3$	$n = 4$
Other student affairs professionals	$n = 1$	$n = 6$	$n = 2$	$n = 4$
Graduate students	$n = 2$	$n = 1$	$n = 1$	$n = 1$

Note. Totals do not add to 100%. Some sections of the same courses are taught by different individuals. Comparisons are between exclusive responsibility versus team approach across same institution types.

$^*p<.05$ $^{**}p<.01$

Table 2.11
Instructional Responsibility for Senior Seminars and Capstone Courses – All Courses by Institution Enrollment Level   (N = 864)

| | Exclusive Responsibility | | | | As Part of a Team | | | |
Instructional Staff	1,000 and Under	1,001-5,000	5,001-10,000	Over 10,000	1,000 and Under	1,001-5,000	5,001-10,000	Over 10,000
Faculty	100	259	81	125	64	105	26	50
Career professionals	8	20	4	5	4	13	2	5
Community leaders	5	7**	5	4**	6	11	4	11
Other	1	5	1	2	0	5	0	2
Other student affairs professionals	2	2*	2	1	0	4	0	2
Graduate students	0	0	0	3	0	0	0	2

Note. Totals do not add to 100%. Some sections of the same courses are taught by different individuals. Comparisons are between exclusive responsibility versus team approach across institutions with same enrollment levels.

$^*p<.05$ $^{**}p<.01$

Table 2.12
Instructional Responsibility for Senior Seminars and Capstone Courses – All Courses by Institution Selectivity (N = 864)

Instructional Staff	Exclusive Responsibility			As Part of a Team		
	High	Medium	Low	High	Medium	Low
Faculty	41	455	69	36	173	36
Career professionals	2	28	7	4	14	6
Community leaders	2	17**	2*	5	22	5
Other	2	6	1	3	4	0
Other student affairs professionals	0	5	2	2	3	1
Graduate students	0	2	1	1	1	0

Note. Totals do not add to 100%. Some sections of the same courses are taught by different individuals. Comparisons are between exclusive responsibility versus team approach across institutions of same selectivity levels.

*p<.05   **p<.01

Respondents representing institutions across selectivity levels noted that community leaders are also asked more often than not to serve on instructional teams (Table 2.12). When offered the opportunity to list "other" instructors, respondents most often described these as guest speakers. Other respondents noted that administrators, adjunct faculty, and academic advisors serve as instructors.

"When offered the opportunity to list 'other' instructors, respondents most often described these as guest speakers."

3. Course Enrollment Levels

The sections of senior seminars and capstone courses described in this survey are small, with 20% of the respondents noting that there are fewer than 10 students in the sections they described (Table 2.13). More than 80% of the respondents noted that sections of the courses enroll fewer than 30 students and only six respondents indicated that the senior seminar or capstone course sections they described enroll 100 or more students. According to these survey results, course sections at public institutions, as noted in Table 2.14, are larger than their private institution counterparts.

Table 2.13
Maximum Section Enrollments in Senior Seminars and Capstone Courses – All Courses (N = 864)

Enrollment Range	Courses
0–9	20.6% (*n* = 178)
10–19	27.4% (*n* = 237)
20–29	33.2% (*n* = 287)
30–39	11.6% (*n* = 100)
40–49	3.4% (*n* = 29)
50–75	3.0% (*n* = 26)
76–99	.1% (*n* = 1)
100+	.8% (*n* = 6)

Table 2.14
Maximum Section Enrollments in Senior Seminars and Capstone Courses – All Courses by Institution Type (N = 864)

	Institution Type	
Enrollment Range	Public (n = 361)	Private (n = 503)
0–9	18.84% (n = 68)	21.8% (n = 110)
10–19	21.3% (n = 77)	31.8% (n = 160)
20–29	35.1% (n = 127)	31.8% (n = 160)
30–39	14.4% (n = 52)	9.5% (n = 48)
40–49	5.2% (n = 19)	1.9% (n = 10)
50–75	4.1% (n = 15)	2.1% (n = 11)
76–99	(0)	.2% (n = 1)
100+	.8% (n = 3)	.6% (n = 3)

"According to this survey, sections of senior seminars and capstone courses at public institutions are larger than their private institution counterparts."

Respondents indicated that course sections at large institutions generally tend to be larger than at institutions of other sizes, although nearly one quarter of the courses at the largest institutions are capped at fewer than 10 students (Table 2.15). Responses indicate that there is little difference between the section size of courses across selectivity level, although nearly 30% of the course sections at highly selective institutions are limited to 10 students, whereas only 17.7% of the course sections at low selectivity institutions are kept to that level (Table 2.16).

Table 2.15

Maximum Section Enrollments in Senior Seminars and Capstone Courses – All Courses by Instituion Enrollment Level (N = 864)

| Enrollment Range | Enrollment Level | | | |
	1,000 and Under (n = 176)	1,001-5,000 (n = 387)	5,001-10,000 (n = 112)	Over 10,000 (n = 189)
0–9	18.7% (n = 33)	19.9% (n = 77)	17.8% (n = 20)	25.4% (n = 48)
10–19	33.3 % (n = 57)	32% (n = 124)	23.2% (n = 26)	15.8% (n = 30)
20–29	32.9% (n = 58)	33.3% (n = 129)	40.1% (n = 45)	29.1% (n = 55)
30–39	9.6% (n = 17)	9.8% (n = 38)	11.6% (n = 13)	16.9% (n = 32)
40–49	3.9% (n = 7)	1.5% (n = 6)	4.4% (n = 5)	5.8% (n = 11)
50–75	1.7% (n = 3)	3.1% (n = 12)	2.6% (n = 3)	4.2% (n = 8)
76–99	.5% (n = 1)	0	0	0
100+	0	.2% (n = 1)	0	2.6% (n = 5)

$p<.01$

"Respondents indicated that course sections at large institutions generally tend to be larger."

Table 2.16

Maximum Section Enrollments in Senior Seminars and Capstone Courses – All Courses by Institution Selectivity (N = 864)

Enrollment Range	Selectivity		
	High (*n* = 81)	Medium (*n* = 670)	Low (*n* = 113)
0–9	29.6% (*n* = 24)	20% (*n* = 134)	17.7% (*n* = 20)
10–19	24.6% (*n* = 22)	27.3% (*n* = 183)	30% (*n* = 34)
20–29	30.8% (*n* = 25)	33.2% (*n* = 223)	34.5% (*n* = 39)
30–39	12.3% (*n* = 10)	11.4% (*n* = 77)	11.5% (*n* = 13)
40–49	1.2% (*n* = 1)	3.4% (*n* = 23)	4.4% (*n* = 5)
50–75	1.2% (*n* = 1)	3.4% (*n* = 23)	1.7% (*n* = 2)
76–99	(0)	.1% (*n* = 1)	(0)
100+	(0)	.9% (*n* = 6)	(0)

4. Amount and Type of Academic Credit and Grading Practices

This survey suggests that the coin of the academic realm, credit, is liberally applied to senior seminars and capstone courses (Table 2.17). More than 20% of respondents indicated that these senior seminars and capstone courses grant four or more semester credits and less than 10% indicated that the courses carry just one semester credit. The number of respondents from quarter credit granting institutions was small. Of those courses that offer this type of credit, more are reported to apply four or more quarter credits to these courses.

Table 2.17

Amount of Credit Granted by Senior Seminars and Capstone Courses – All Courses (N = 780)

	Courses	
Credit Hours	Number	Percentage
One qtr.	8	1.0%
Two qtrs.	3	0.4%
Three qtrs.	5	0.6%
Four qtrs.	12	1.5%
Five qtrs.	8	1.0%
Six or more qtrs.	6	0.8%
One sem.	74	9.5%
Two sems.	54	6.9%
Three sems.	450	57.7%
Four or more sems.	160	20.5%

Table 2.18
Amount of Credit Granted by Senior Seminars and Capstone Courses – All Courses by Institution Type (N = 780)

Credit Hours	Institution Type	
	Public	Private
One qtr.	.1% (n = 1)	1.5% (n = 7)
Two qtrs.	(0)	.6% (n = 3)
Three qtrs.	.6% (n = 2)	.6% (n = 3)
Four qtrs.	1.2% (n = 4)	1.7% (n = 8)
Five qtrs.	2.4% (n = 8)	(0)
Six or more qtrs.	.9% (n = 3)	.6% (n = 3)
One sem.	7.8% (n = 26)	10.7% (n = 48)
Two sems.	4.2% (n = 14)	8.9% (n = 40)
Three sems.	64.4% (n = 214)	52.68% (n – 236)
Four or more sems.	18% (n = 60)	22.1% (n = 99)

p<.01

The practices between public and private institutions and among institutions of the three selectivity levels are somewhat different (Tables 2.18 and 2.20), with more private institutions offering semester credit and highly selective institutions offering four or more semester credits. However, this difference may be attributed to a larger number of public institutions and institutions of medium and low selectivity offering courses in a quarter credit system.

Responses indicate little difference in these practices across enrollment levels (Table 2.19).

Table 2.19

Amount of Credit Granted by Senior Seminars and Capstone Courses – All Courses by Institution Enrollment Level (N = 780)

Credit Hours	Enrollment Level			
	1,000 and Under	1,001-5,000	5,001-10,000	Over 10,000
One qtr.	1.2% (n = 2)	1.4% (n = 5)	.9% (n = 1)	(0)
Two qtrs.	(0)	.2% (n = 1)	(0)	1.1% (n = 2)
Three qtrs.	.6% (n = 1)	.5% (n = 2)	.9% (n = 1)	.5% (n = 1)
Four qtrs.	(0)	1.7% (n = 6)	.9% (n = 1)	1.7% (n = 3)
Five qtrs.	(0)	.8% (n = 3)	.9% (n = 1)	2.3% (n = 4)
Six or more qtrs.	(0)	.5% (n = 2)	(0)	2.3% (n = 4)
One sem.	8.1% (n = 13)	11.4% (n = 40)	9.8% (n = 10)	6.4% (n = 11)
Two sems.	11.3% (n = 18)	5.4% (n = 19)	4.9% (n = 5)	7% (n = 12)
Three sems.	59.1% (n = 94)	53.1% (n = 185)	66.6% (n = 68)	60.2% (n = 103)
Four or more sems.	17.6% (n = 28)	24.4% (n = 85)	14.7% (n = 15)	18.1% (n = 31)

Table 2.20
*Amount of Credit Granted by Senior Seminars and Capstone
Courses – All Courses by Institution Selectivity (N = 780)*

| | Selectivity | | |
Credit Hours	High	Medium	Low
One qtr.	1.4% (n = 1)	.9% (n = 6)	1% (n = 1)
Two qtrs.	(0)	.4% (n = 3)	(0)
Three qtrs.	(0)	.6% (n = 4)	1% (n = 1)
Four qtrs.	2.8% (n = 2)	1.1% (n = 7)	3% (n = 3)
Five qtrs.	1.4% (n = 1)	.8% (n = 5)	2% (n = 2)
Six or more qtrs.	2.8% (n = 2)	.6% (n = 4)	(0)
One sems.	12.8% (n = 9)	9.1% (n = 56)	9% (n = 9)
Two sems.	2.8% (n = 2)	6.3% (n = 39)	13% (n = 13)
Three sems.	38.7% (n = 27)	60.3% (n = 368)	55% (n = 55)
Four or more sems.	37.1% (n = 26)	19.3% (n = 118)	15% (n = 15)

p<.01

As indicated by these survey respondents, the type of credit applied to these courses suggest that they are an integral component of degree programs. Only 39 respondents (4.5%) said the courses they described do not grant credit and just 64 respondents (7.4%) said these courses are graded pass/fail.

Nearly 90% of the respondents said these courses are offered as part of the institutions' core requirements or as major requirements. Consistent with the focus away from general education, only 5.3% of respondents said the courses fulfill general education requirements. These credit granting practices do not vary widely across types, enrollment, and selectivity levels of institutions (Table 2.21 through Table 2.24).

Table 2.21

Type of Credit Granted by Senior Seminars and Capstone Courses – All Courses (N = 864)

Granting Credit	Number	Percentage
Yes	825	95.4%
No	39	4.5%

Type of Grade	Number	Percentage
Pass/fail	64	7.4%
Letter grade	800	92.5%

Type of Credit	Number	Percentage
Core requirement	211	24.4%
Elective	43	4.9%
Major requirement	539	62.3%
General education requirement	46	5.3%
Other	25	2.8%

"Only 39 respondents (4.5%) said the courses they described do not grant credit..."

Table 2.22
Type of Credit Granted by Senior Seminars and Capstone Courses –
All Courses by Institution Type (N = 864)

	Institution Type	
Granting Credit	Public	Private
Yes	95.8% (*n* = 346)	95.2% (*n* = 479)
No	4.1% (*n* = 15)	4.7% (*n* = 24)

	Institution Type	
Type of Grade	Public	Private
Pass/fail	7.76% (*n* = 28)	7.16% (*n* =36)
Letter grade	92.2% (*n* = 333)	92.8% (*n* = 467)

	Institution Type	
Credit Applied As	Public	Private
Core requirement	22.1% (*n* = 80)	26% (*n* = 131)
Elective	5.2% (*n* = 19)	4.7% (*n* = 24)
Major requirement	63.7% (*n* = 230)	61.4% (*n* = 309)
General education requirement	5.5% (*n* = 20)	5.1% (*n* = 26)
Other	3.3% (*n* = 12)	2.5% (*n* = 13)

"…only 5.3% of respondents said the courses
fulfill general education requirements."

Of those respondents who noted that these courses grant "other" types of credits, most indicated that the courses are offered as honors requirements. Other respondents noted that the courses they were describing carry non-degree credit and credit for certification and minor degrees.

Table 2.23

Type of Credit Granted by Senior Seminars and Capstone Courses – All Courses by Institution Enrollment Level (N = 864)

Granting Credit	Enrollment Level			
	1,000 and Under	1,001-5,000	5,001-10,000	Over 10,000
Yes	96% (n = 169)	95.8% (n = 371)	94.6% (n = 106)	94.7% (n = 179)
No	3.9% (n = 7)	4.1% (n = 16)	5.3% (n = 6)	5.2% (n = 10)

Type of Grade	Enrollment Level			
	1,000 and Under	1,001-5,000	5,001-10,000	Over 10,000
Pass/fail	6.8% (n = 12)	7.4% (n = 29)	8.9% (n = 10)	6.8% (n = 13)
Letter grade	93.1% (n = 164)	92.5% (n = 358)	91% (n = 102)	93.1% (n = 176)

Credit Applied As	Enrollment Level			
	1,000 and under	1,001-5,000	5,001-10,000	Over 10,000
Core requirement	34% (n = 60)	21.1% (n = 82)	21.4% (n = 24)	23.8% (n = 45)
Elective	2.8% (n = 5)	5.1% (n = 20)	3.5% (n = 4)	7.4% (n = 14)
Major requirement	53.4% (n = 94)	66.4% (n = 257)	65.1% (n = 73)	60.8% (n = 115)
General education requirement	6.8% (n = 12)	4.9% (n = 19)	7.1% (n = 8)	3.7% (n = 7)
Other	2.8% (n = 5)	2.3% (n = 9)	2.6% (n = 3)	4.2% (n = 8)

Table 2.24

*Type of Credit Granted by Senior Seminars and Capstone Courses –
All Courses by Institution Selectivity (N = 864)*

	Selectivity		
	High	Medium	Low
Granting Credit			
Yes	92.5% (*n* = 75)	95.7% (*n* = 643)	94.6% (*n* = 107)
No	7.4% (*n* = 6)	4% (*n* = 27)	5.3% (*n* = 6)

	Selectivity		
	High	Medium	Low
Type of Grade			
Pass/fail	7.4% (*n* = 6)	7.7% (*n* = 52)	5.3% (*n* = 6)
Letter grade	92.5% (*n* = 75)	92.2% (*n* = 618)	94.6% (*n* = 107)

	Selectivity		
	High	Medium	Low
Credit Applied As			
Core requirement	17.2% (*n* = 14)	23.7% (*n* = 159	33.6% (*n* = 38)
Elective	8.6% (*n* = 7)	4.9% (*n* = 33)	2.6% (*n* = 3)
Major requirement	64.2% (*n* = 52)	62.9% (*n* = 422)	57.5% (*n* = 65)
General education requirement	6.1% (*n* = 5)	5.5% (*n* = 37)	3.5% (*n* = 4)
Other	3.7% (*n* = 3)	2.8% (*n* = 19)	2.6% (*n* = 3)

5. Length of Course

This survey suggests that nearly all senior seminars and capstone courses are at least one semester in length, with more than 10% of respondents indicating that these courses are offered over two academic terms, either quarters or semesters (Table 2.25). Courses at private institutions are reportedly longer than those at their public institution counterparts (Tables 2.26 and 2.27).

Table 2.25
Length of Senior Seminars and Capstone Courses – All Courses (N = 819)

Length of Courses	Percentage and Number
1-8 weeks	3.2% (n = 26)
1 quarter	4.5% (n = 37)
1 semester	81.9% (n = 671)
2 quarters	1.2% (n = 10)
2 semesters	9.2% (n = 75)

Table 2.26
Length of Senior Seminars and Capstone Courses – All Courses by Institution Type (N = 819)

	Institution Type	
Length of Courses	Public	Private
1-8 weeks	1.7% (n = 6)	4.2% (n = 20)
1 quarter	4.3% (n = 15)	4.6% (n = 22)
1 semester	86.4% (n = 300)	78.6% (n = 371)
2 quarters	1.4% (n = 5)	1% (n = 5)
2 semesters	6% (n = 28)	11.4% (n = 54)

Table 2.27
Length of Senior Seminars and Capstone Courses – All Courses by Institution Enrollment Level (N = 819)

Length of Course	Enrollment Level			
	1,000 and Under	1,001-5,000	5,001-10,000	Over 10,000
1-8 weeks	5.4% (n = 9)	2.7% (n = 10)	1.8% (n = 2)	2.8% (n = 5)
1 quarter	2.4% (n = 4)	4.6% (n = 17)	4.6% (n = 5)	6.2% (n = 11)
1 semester	81.3% (n = 135)	82.9% (n = 306)	87% (n = 94)	77.2% (n = 136)
2 quarters	.60% (n = 1)	1% (n = 4)	.93% (n = 1)	2.2% (n = 4)
2 semesters	10.2% (n = 17)	8.6% (n = 32)	5.5% (n = 6)	11.3% (n = 20)

Table 2.28
Length of Senior Seminars and Capstone Courses – All Courses by Institution Selectivity (N = 819)

Length of Course	Selectivity		
	High	Medium	Low
1-8 weeks	1.3% (n = 1)	3.4% (n = 22)	2.7% (n = 3)
1 quarter	5.4% (n = 4)	4.2% (n = 27)	5.5% (n = 6)
1 semester	71.2% (n = 52)	82.7% (n = 527)	84.4% (n = 92)
2 quarters	5.4% (n = 4)	.94% (n = 6)	(0)
2 semesters	16.4% (n = 12)	8.6% (n = 55)	.98% (n = 8)

$p<.05$

Courses at highly selective institutions are reportedly twice as likely to be two semesters in length than those at medium selectivity institutions and less than 1% of respondents indicated that courses at low selectivity institutions are two semesters long (Table 2.28).

6. Administrative Responsibility

The survey instrument allowed respondents to describe, in narrative, which academic unit administers senior seminars and capstone courses. Nearly all are reported to be administered by individual academic departments. Among the handful of other units administering the courses were career service centers, academic affairs, student affairs, general education and honors programs.

7. Instructional Practices

Respondents were asked to mark all instructional components that apply to the courses they described, therefore the responses in this section are not mutually exclusive. Through each type of analysis, oral presentation was consistently rated the primary instructional approach, with major project following closely behind (Tables 2.29 through 2.32).

Table 2.29

Senior Seminar and Capstone Course Instructional Components – All Courses (N = 864)

Instructional Component	Frequency of Use (In Descending Order)	
	Number	Percentage
Oral presentation	649	75.1%
Major project	621	71.9%
Group project	390	45.1%
Final exam	343	39.7%
Portfolio development	320	37.0%
Thesis	234	27.1%
Use of career center	143	16.6%
Internship	131	15.2%
Other	128	14.8%
Explicit consideration of graduate school	120	13.9%
Alumni involvement/networking	117	13.5%
Leadership training	100	11.6%
Service learning/community service	93	10.8%
Educational travel	40	4.6%
Employment (remunerative/non-remunerative)	30	3.5%
Work shadowing	28	3.2%

Note. Totals do not add to 100%. Respondents were asked to mark all that apply.

Table 2.30
*Senior Seminar and Capstone Course Instructional Components –
All Courses by Institution Type (N = 864)*

Instructional Component	Frequency of Use by Institution Type	
	Public	Private
Oral presentation	75.6% (*n* = 273)	74.7% (*n* = 376)
Major project	75.3% (*n* = 272)	69.3% (*n* = 349)
Group project	53.1% (*n* = 192) **	39.3% (*n* = 198)
Final exam	46.5% (*n* = 168) **	34.7% (*n* = 175)
Portfolio development	40.4% (*n* = 145)	34.5% (*n* = 174)
Thesis	19.6% (*n* = 71) **	32.4% (*n* = 163)
Use of career center	19.1% (*n* = 69)	14.7% (*n* = 74)
Internship	12.4% (*n* = 45)	17.1% (*n* = 86)
Other	14.1% (*n* = 51)	15.3% (*n* = 77)
Explicit consideration of graduate school	13% (*n* = 47)	14.5% (*n* = 73)
Alumni involvement/networking	14.6% (*n* = 53)	12.7% (*n* = 64)
Leadership training	12.9% (*n* = 44)	11.1% (*n* = 56)
Service learning/community service	11.3% (*n* = 41)	10.3% (*n* = 52)
Educational travel	4.1% (*n* = 15)	4.9% (*n* = 25)
Employment (remunerative/non-remunerative)	2.2% (*n* = 8)	4.3% (*n* = 22)
Work shadowing	3.3% (*n* = 12)	3.1% (*n* = 16)

Note. Totals do not add to 100%. Respondents were asked to mark all that apply.

**p<.01

The least frequently indicated instructional techniques were those taking students out of the classroom, including service learning, educational travel, employment, and work shadowing. Courses at public institutions are more likely to require final examinations and group projects than those at private institutions, while courses at private institutions are more likely to require a senior thesis (Table 2.30).

"The least frequently indicated instructional techniques were those taking students out of the classroom..."

Selection of group project as an instructional technique is positively correlated with size of institution, while thesis use, with one exception, negatively correlates with institution size (Table 2.31).

Table 2.31

Senior Seminar and Capstone Course Instructional Components – All Courses by Institution Enrollment Level (N = 864)

Instructional Component	Frequency of Use by Enrollment Level			
	1,000 and Under	1,001-5,000	5,001-10,000	Over 10,000
Oral presentation	77.2% (n = 136)	75.9% (n = 294)	75.8% (n = 85)	70.9% (n = 134)
Major project	67% (n = 118)	72.3% (n = 280)	72.3% (n = 81)	75.1% (n = 142)
Group project	36.9% (n = 65)*	44.4% (n = 172)	49.1% (n 55)	51.8% (n = 98)
Final exam	35.8% (n = 63)	38.7% (n = 150)	42.8% (n = 48)	43.3% (n = 82)
Portfolio development	39.2% (n = 69)	37.4% (n = 145)	41% (n = 46)	31.7 (n = 60)
Thesis	30.6% (n = 54)**	31% (n = 120)	21.4% (n = 24)	19% (n = 36)
Use of career center	14.2% (n = 25)	17.3% (n = 67)	18.7% (n = 21)	15.8% (n = 30)
Internship	17.6% (n = 31)	15.7% (n = 61)	15.1% (n = 17)	11.6% (n = 22)
Other	17% (n = 30)	12.6% (n = 49)	19.6% (n = 22)	14.2% (n = 27)
Explicit consideration of graduate school	16.4% (n = 29)	13.7% (n = 53)	16.9% (n = 19)	10% (n = 19)
Alumni involvement/ networking	10.8% (n = 19)	13.7% (n = 53)	12.5% (n = 14)	16.4% (n = 31)
Leadership training	11.9% (n = 21)	9.8% (n = 38)	10.7% (n = 12)	15.3% (n = 29)
Service learning/ community service	9% (n = 16)	11.8% (n = 46)	9.8% (n = 11)	10.5% (n = 20)
Educational travel	2.8% (n = 5)	4.3% (n = 17)	4.4% (n = 5)	6.8% (n = 13)
Employment (remunerative/ non-remunerative)	.5% (n = 8)	3.8% (n = 15)	1.7% (n = 2)	2.6% (n = 5)
Work shadowing	3.4% (n = 6)	2.5% (n = 10)	5.3% (n = 6)	3.1% (n = 6)

Note. Totals do not add to 100%. Respondents were asked to mark all that apply.

*p<.05   ** p<.01

Table 2.32

*Senior Seminar and Capstone Course Instructional Components –
All Courses by Institution Selectivity (N = 864)*

Instructional Component	Frequency of Use by Selectivity		
	High	Medium	Low
Oral presentation	74% (n = 60)	75.5% (n = 506)	73.4% (n = 83)
Major project	70.3% (n = 57)	71.9% (n = 482)	72.5% (n = 82)
Group project	39.5% (n = 32)	46.5% (n = 312)	40.7% (n = 46)
Final exam	29.6% (n = 24)	40.9% (n = 274)	39.8% (n = 45)
Portfolio development	33.3% (n = 27)	37.4% (n = 251)	37.1% (n = 42)
Thesis	43.2% (n = 35)**	26.7% (n = 179)	17.7% (n = 20)
Use of career center	11.1% (n = 9)	17.3% (n = 116)	15.9% (n = 18)
Internship	11.1% (n = 9)	15.2% (n = 102)	17.7% (n = 20)
Other	17.2% (n = 14)	15.5% (n = 104)	8.8% (n = 10)
Explicit consideration of graduate school	14.8% (n = 12)	14.7% (n = 99)	7.9% (n = 9)
Alumni involvement/networking	12.3% (n = 10)	14.6% (n = 98)	7.9% (n = 9)
Leadership training	8.6% (n = 7)	11% (n = 74)	16.8% (n = 19)
Service learning/community service	8.6% (n = 7)	11% (n = 74)	10.6% (n = 12)
Educational travel	3.7% (n = 3)	4.9% (n = 33)	3.5% (n = 4)
Employment (remunerative/non-remunerative)	3.7% (n = 3)	3.1% (n = 21)	5.3% (n = 6)
Work shadowing	3.7% (n = 3)	2.6% (n = 18)	6.1% (n = 7)

Note. Totals do not add to 100%. Respondents were asked to mark all that apply.

**$p<.01$

As noted in Table 2.32, a positive correlation exists between selectivity and the requirement of a thesis in senior seminars and capstone courses. Responses indicate that courses at low selectivity institutions are less likely to include as an instructional technique exploring graduate school and involving alumni, and are more likely to include opportunities for work shadowing, although the differences are not statistically significant and in most instances the number of responses is small.

Additional instructional components listed as "other" by respondents included job interviews, resume' writing, fine arts performances, exhibitions, case studies, research projects, and standardized tests.

8. Populations Required to Take the Course

Nearly 70% of respondents to this survey indicated that senior seminars and capstone courses are required, not elective, courses (Table 2.33). This holds true across institutional types and institutional enrollment and selectivity levels, with two exceptions (Tables 2.34 through 2.36).

Table 2.33
Students Required to Take Senior Seminars and Capstone Courses –
All Courses (N = 864)

Students Required to Take Course	Number	Percentage
All	604	69.9%
Some	219	25.3%
None	41	4.7%

Table 2.34
Students Required to Take Senior Seminars and Capstone Courses –
All Courses by Institution Type (N = 864)

	Institution Type	
Students Required to Take Course	Public	Private
All	68.7% (*n* = 248)	70.7% (*n* = 356)
Some	26% (*n* = 94)	24.8% (*n* = 125)
None	5.2% (*n* = 19)	4.3% (*n* = 22)

"Nearly 70% of respondents to this survey indicated that senior seminars and capstone courses are required..."

Table 2.35
Students Required to Take Senior Seminars and Capstone Courses –
All Courses by Institution Enrollment Level (N = 864)

Students Required to Take Course	Enrollment Level			
	1,000 and Under	1,001-5,000	5,001-10,000	Over 10,000
All	72.1% (*n* = 127)	70.8% (*n* = 274)	71.4% (*n* = 80)	65% (*n* = 123)
Some	25.5% (*n* = 45)	23.7% (*n* = 92)	25% (*n* = 28)	28.5% (*n* = 54)
None	2.2% (*n* = 4)	5.4% (*n* = 21)	3.5% (*n* = 4)	6.3% (*n* = 12)

Table 2.36
Students Required to Take Senior Seminars and Capstone Courses –
All Courses by Institution Selectivity (N = 864)

Students Required to Take Course	Selectivity		
	High	Medium	Low
All	58% (*n* = 47)	70.9% (*n* = 475)	72.5% (*n* = 82)
Some	33.3% (*n* = 27)	24.6% (*n* = 165)	23.8% (*n* = 27)
None	8.6% (*n* = 7)	4.4% (*n* = 30)	3.5% (*n* = 4)

The responses indicate that students in courses at the largest institutions are less likely to be required to enroll in these courses (Table 2.35), as are students in courses at highly selective institutions (Table 2.36). However, these differences are not statistically significant.

The survey instrument also allowed respondents to describe the gender ratio of students who take these courses when they are offered as electives (Tables 2.37 through 2.40). Respondents reported that women are more likely than men to enroll in these courses voluntarily.

Table 2.37
Gender Ratio of Senior Seminars and Capstone Courses – All Courses (N = 126)

| | Courses | |
Gender Ratio	Number	Percentage
70% women	20	15.9%
50 – 70% women	45	35.7%
50/50	30	23.8%
50 – 70% men	21	16.7%
70% men	10	7.9%

Note. Applies only to elective courses.

Table 2.38
Gender Ratio of Senior Seminars and Capstone Courses – All Courses by Institution Type (N = 126)

| | Institution Type | |
Gender Ratio	Public	Private
70% women	16% ($n = 9$)	15.7% ($n = 11$)
50 – 70% women	32.1% ($n = 18$)	38.5% ($n = 27$)
50/50	19.6% ($n = 11$)	27.1% ($n = 19$)
50 – 70% men	23.2% ($n = 13$)	11.4% ($n = 8$)
70% men	8.9% ($n = 5$)	7.1% ($n = 5$)

Note. Applies only to elective courses.

Table 2.39

Gender Ratio of Senior Seminars and Capstone Courses – All Courses by Institution Enrollment Level (N = 126)

Gender Ratio	Enrollment Level			
	1,000 and Under	1,001-5,000	5,001-10,000	Over 10,000
70% women	22.7% (n = 5)	18.9% (n = 11)	11.7% (n = 2)	6.9% (n = 2)
50 – 70% women	27.7% (n = 6)	36.2% (n = 21)	52.9% (n = 9)	31% (n = 9)
50/50	36.6% (n = 8)	17.2% (n = 10)	23.5% (n = 4)	27.5% (n = 8)
50 – 70% men	9% (n = 2)	20.6% (n = 12)	5.8% (n = 1)	20.6% (n = 6)
70% men	4.5% (n = 1)	6.9% (n = 4)	5.8% (n = 1)	13.7% (n = 4)

Note. Applies only to elective courses.

Table 2.40

Gender Ratio of Senior Seminars and Capstone Courses – All Courses by Institution Selectivity (N = 126)

Gender Ratio	Selectivity		
	High	Medium	Low
70% women	(0)	19.7% (n = 19)	5.2% (n = 1)
50 – 70% women	36.6% (n = 4)	36.4% (n = 35)	31.5% (n = 6)
50/50	45.5% (n = 5)	22.9% (n = 22)	15.7% (n = 3)
50 – 70% men	(0)	12.5% (n = 12)	47.3% (n = 9)
70% men	18.8% (n = 2)	8.3% (n = 8)	(0)

Note. Applies only to elective courses.

$p<.01$

One explanation for a larger presence of females might have been a disproportionate representation in the response population of institutions traditionally enrolling females. However, a review of the 126 respondents answering this question revealed that none were reporting from single gender institutions.

9. Length of Existence at the Institution

Of the 703 respondents completing the section on the length of time senior seminars and capstone courses have existed at their institutions, the highest number indicated that these courses were less than 15 years old (Table 2.41).

Table 2.41

Length of Existence at Institution of Senior Seminars and Capstone Courses — All Courses (N = 703)

Range of Years	Number	Percentage
< 1	6	.9%
1–5	232	33%
6–10	174	24.8%
11–15	95	13.5%
16–20	84	11.9%
21–25	45	6.4%
26–30	38	5.4%
31–35	10	1.4%
36–40	8	1.1%
41–45	2	.3%
46–50	5	.7%
51–78	4	.7%

Table 2.42
Length of Existence at Institution of Senior Seminars and Capstone Courses – All Courses by Institution Type (N = 703)

| Range of Years | Institution Type | |
	Public	Private
< 1	.34% (*n* = 1)	1.2% (*n* = 5)
1–5	31.1% (*n* = 91)	34.31% (*n* = 141)
6–10	25.3% (*n* = 74)	24.3% (*n* = 100)
11–15	14% (*n* = 41)	13.1% (*n* = 54)
16–20	12.6% (*n*= 37)	11.4% (*n* = 47)
21–25	8.9% (*n* = 26	4.6% (*n* = 19)
26–30	5.4% (*n* = 16)	5.3% (*n* = 22)
31–35	1% (*n* = 3)	1.7% (*n* = 7)
36–40	(0)	1.9% (*n* = 8)
41–45	(0)	.49% (*n* = 2)
46–50	.34% (*n* = 1)	.97% (*n* = 4)
51–78	.68% (*n* = 2)	.49% (*n* = 2)

The most frequent response (33%) was that these courses are between one and five years old. Courses at public and private (Table 2.42), large and small (Table 2.43), and high, medium, and low selectivity level institutions (Table 2.44) are similar in age.

Table 2.43

Length of Existence at Institution of Senior Seminars and Capstone Courses – All Courses by Institution Enrollment Level (N = 703)

	Enrollment Level			
Range of Years	1,000 and Under	1,001-5,000	5,001-10,000	Over 10,000
< 1	1.3% (n = 2)	.96% (n = 3)	(0)	.68% (n = 1)
1–5	33.3% (n = 51)	34.7% (n = 108)	28.2% (n = 26)	31.9% (n = 47)
6–10	26.1% (n = 40)	24.1% (n = 75)	21.7% (n = 20)	26.5% (n = 39)
11–15	11.7% (n = 18)	13.1% (n = 41)	18.4% (n = 17)	12.9% (n = 19)
16–20	9.8% (n = 15)	11.2% (n = 35)	16.3% (n = 15)	12.9% (n = 19)
21–25	8.5% (n = 13)	5.7% (n = 18)	9.7% (n = 9)	3.4% (n = 5)
26–30	4.5% (n = 7)	4.8% (n = 15)	3.2% (n = 3)	8.8% (n = 13)
31–35	.65% (n – 1)	1.9% (n – 6)	1% (n – 1)	1.3% (n = 2)
36–40	2.6% (n = 4)	1.2% (n = 4)	(0)	(0)
41–45	(0)	.32% (n = 1)	1% (n = 1)	(0)
46–50	1.3% (n = 2)	.64% (n = 2)	(0)	.68% (n = 1)
51–78	(0)	.96% (n = 3)	(0)	.68% (n = 1)

Table 2.44
Length of Existence at Institution of Senior Seminars and Capstone Courses – All Courses by Institution Selectivity (N = 703)

| | Selectivity | | |
Range of Years	High	Medium	Low
< 1	1.7% (*n* = 1)	.54% (*n* = 3)	2.2% (*n* = 2)
1–5	21% (*n* = 12)	33.1% (*n* = 184)	39.5% (*n* = 36)
6–10	21% (*n* = 12)	24.6% (*n* = 137)	27.4% (*n* = 25)
11–15	8.7% (*n* = 5)	15.3% (*n* = 85)	5.4% (*n* = 5)
16–20	19.3% (*n* = 11)	11.1% (*n* = 62)	12% (*n* = 11)
21–25	14% (*n* = 8)	5.5% (*n* = 31)	6.5% (*n* = 6)
26–30	7% (*n* = 4)	5.4% (*n* = 30)	4.4% (*n* = 4)
31–35	3.5% (*n* = 2)	1.4% (*n* = 8)	(0)
36–40	1.7% (*n* = 1)	.9% (*n* = 5)	2.2% (*n* = 2)
41–45	(0)	.36% (*n* = 2)	(0)
46–50	1.7% (*n* = 1)	.72% (*n* = 4)	(0)
51–78	(0)	.72 (*n* = 4)	(0)

10. Evaluation Practices

Most respondents indicated that students and individual faculty members evaluate the courses. To a lesser extent, respondents reported that evaluations are conducted by the department offering the course, central administrators, curriculum committees, self-study committees, and accrediting bodies. More than 20% of the respondents noted that the courses they described are not evaluated in any manner, with this holding true across institution type (Table 2.45 and 2.46).

Table 2.45
Evaluation of Senior Seminars and Capstone Courses – All Courses (N = 864)

Course Evaluated	Number	Percentage
Yes	688	79.6%
No	176	20.3%

Note. Majority of courses evaluated by students enrolled.

Table 2.46
Evaluation of Senior Seminars and Capstone Courses – All Courses by Institution Type (N = 864)

	Institution Type	
Course Evaluated	Public	Private
Yes	78.1% (n = 282)	80.72% (n = 406)
No	21.8% (n = 79)	19.2% (n = 97)

Note. Majority of courses evaluated by students enrolled.

Table 2.47
Evaluation of Senior Seminars and Capstone Courses – All Courses by Institution Enrollment Level (N = 864)

	Enrollment Level			
Course Evaluated	1,000 and Under	1,001-5,000	5,001-10,000	Over 10,000
Yes	83.5% (n = 147)	78.8% (n = 305)	82.1% (n = 92)	76.1% (n = 144)
No	16.4% (n = 29)	21.1% (n = 82)	17.8% (n = 20)	23.8 (n = 45)

Note. Majority of courses evaluated by students enrolled.

Table 2.48

Evaluation of Senior Seminars and Capstone Courses – All Courses by Institution Selectivity (N = 864)

	Selectivity		
Course Evaluated	High	Medium	Low
Yes	81.4% (*n* = 66)	78% (*n* = 537)	75.2% (*n* = 85)
No	18.5% (*n* = 15)	19.8% (*n* = 133)	24.7% (*n* = 28)

Note. Majority of courses evaluated by students enrolled.

According to this survey, courses at the smallest (under 1,000 students) and next to largest (enrollments between 5,001 to 10,000) institutions are more likely to be evaluated than those at institutions with enrollments of between 1,001 to 5,000 and over 10,000 (Table 2.47). There is a slight positive correlation between institutional selectivity and existence of evaluation, with courses at more selective institutions being evaluated at a greater rate (Table 2.48).

"There is a slight positive correlation between institutional selectivity and existence of evaluation..."

11. Assessment Practices

More than half of the respondents indicated that the senior seminars and capstone courses they were describing are not part of formal institutional assessments (Table 2.49).

Those courses at private institutions and small institutions are more likely to be folded into institutional assessments (Tables 2.50 and 2.51).

Table 2.49
Assessment Tied to Senior Seminars and Capstone Courses – All Courses (N = 864)

Course Linked to Comprehensive Assessment	Number	Percentage
Yes	400	46.2%
No	464	53.7%

Table 2.50
Assessment Tied to Senior Seminars and Capstone Courses – All Courses by Institution Type (N = 864)

Course Linked to Comprehensive Assessment	Institution Type	
	Public	Private
Yes	41.2% ($n = 149$)	49.9% ($n = 251$)
No	58.7% ($n = 212$)	50.1% ($n = 252$)

$p<.05$

"More than half of the respondents indicated that the senior seminars and capstone courses they were describing are not part of formal institutional assessments."

Table 2.51
Assessment Tied to Senior Seminars and Capstone Courses – All Courses by Institution Enrollment Level (N = 864)

Course Linked to Comprehensive Assessment	Enrollment Level			
	1,000 and Under	1,001-5,000	5,001-10,000	Over 10,000
Yes	64.7% (n = 114)	47% (n = 182)	36.6% (n = 41)	33.3% (n = 63)
No	35.2% (n = 62)	52.9% (n = 205)	63.3% (n = 71)	66.6% (n = 126)

p<.05

Table 2.52
Assessment Tied to Senior Seminars and Senior Courses – All Courses by Institution Selectivity Level (N = 864)

Course Linked to Comprehensive Assessment	Selectivity		
	High	Medium	Low
Yes	38.2% (n = 31)	44.9% (n = 301)	60.1% (n = 68)
No	61.7% (n = 50)	55% (n = 369)	39.8% (n = 45)

p<.01

Nearly 65% of the respondents indicated that senior seminars and capstone courses from small institutions are included in these assessments, while that number is just over 30% for courses at the largest institutions. The lower the selectivity of an institution, the greater the likelihood that the course will be assessed, reversing the evaluation pattern indicated above (Table 2.52).

Some 376 respondents described a wide variety of techniques used to assess senior seminars and capstone courses at three institutional and extra-institutional levels, i.e., within academic departments, centrally, and by statewide entities. Departmental assessment is conducted through portfolios, exit interviews, surveys, and pre- and post-testing of students. Centrally, some courses are assessed by general education units. Extra-institutionally, courses are assessed through accreditation processes and external reviews.

"The lower the selectivity of an institution, the greater the likelihood that the course will be assessed..."

Summary of Analysis – All Courses

Results of this survey suggest that college and university seniors who enroll in senior seminars and capstone courses are most likely to culminate learning in their academic major. This ending academic experience most frequently includes completion by the student of a major project and delivery of an oral presentation to student colleagues and an individual academic faculty member who teaches the course. Responses indicate that academic departments offering the courses described in this survey most frequently require students to enroll in them before they graduate and reward them for doing so with a high number of academic credits.

This survey suggests that institutions share similar number one goals for these senior seminars and capstone courses. Along with capping the academic major, they are, secondarily, intended to prepare students for the world of work through classroom-based assignments and activities. Especially at medium selectivity institutions, the courses described by respondents are not meant to recall the learning students have done prior to the academic major in the general education curriculum. Respondents indicated that the courses they described give lowest priority to any experience that takes seniors out of the classroom. Graduate students and student affairs professionals outside career centers are reported to be least likely to be asked to teach these courses, while community leaders are sometimes asked to serve on instructional teams.

As described by survey respondents, sections of senior seminars and capstone courses at large and public institutions have somewhat greater numbers of students enrolled in them than those at small and private institutions. However, nearly all of these courses cap section enrollments at fewer than 30 students. Highly selective institutions are somewhat more likely to grant a greater number of credits for these courses than other institutions and nearly all respondents indicated that academic departments administer senior seminars and capstone courses. Along with the ubiquitous oral presentation and major project, a thesis is reported to be more likely to be required of students in courses at private and small institutions, while final examinations and group projects are more likely to be part of courses at public and larger institutions. While respondents suggested that most of these courses are evaluated, fewer than half of them are folded into comprehensive assessment efforts.

Chapter 3

Survey Results for Discipline- and Department-based Courses

Chapter 3 is divided into three sections. The first section offers a display of results and analysis of discipline- and department-based senior seminars and capstone courses by the three key variables (institution type, institution enrollment level, and institution selectivity level) across 11 components of these courses (as listed in Chapter 1). The second section offers a summary of analysis for the first section and the final section summarizes findings for these courses by discipline cluster. As indicated in Chapter 1, the nine clusters used to categorize data on discipline- and department-based courses are derived from those created by the American Council on Education. They include:

1. Biological sciences
2. Business and management
3. Education
4. Engineering
5. Humanities
6. Journalism and communications
7. Nursing
8. Physical sciences and mathematics
9. Social sciences

In total, 285 responses were returned, each indicating a link between the course described and one of these nine discipline clusters. The other 322 respondents who indicated they were reporting on discipline- or department-based senior seminar or capstone courses did not specify ties to specific disciplines.

With 607 total returned forms, responses on discipline- and department-based senior seminars and capstone courses comprised the largest group of responses on course types in this survey. However, in several respects, most of the rest of the courses under other course types, as they were described by survey respondents, share characteristics with these discipline- and department-based courses. For example, when analyzed separately, data across all course types, as reported in this chapter, Chapter 4 and 5, indicate that the primary goals of most of these courses are chiefly to foster integration and synthesis within the academic major and to prepare students for the world of work. When analyzed separately by course type, responses suggest that most of these courses are taught by faculty members working alone, that most instructors teaching these courses require students to prepare oral presentations and complete major projects, that most of these courses are administered by single academic departments, that most of these courses are evaluated by the faculty and students involved in them, and that most are not involved in comprehensive assessment. The result is that, analyzed together and separately, responses from this survey indicate that most interdisciplinary, career planning, transition, and other courses are more like discipline- and department-based senior seminars and capstone courses than they are different from them. Nonetheless, respondents did report important differences across and within these course types. In many instances, for example, some courses at public institutions are reported to be taught differently than those at private institutions, differences appear to exist between courses taught at various sizes of institutions, and selectivity of institution appears to make some difference. Both the similarities and differences across key variables, course types, and course components are noteworthy.

A baseline for understanding these similarities and differences is appropriately set by reviewing results of discipline- and department-based senior seminars and capstone courses. Tables 3.1, 3.2, 3.3, and 3.4 offer the percentages for discipline clusters by institution type, institution enrollment and institution selectivity levels.

Table 3.1

Total Number and Percentage of Discipline- or Department-based Courses by Discipline Cluster (N = 285)

Discipline Cluster	Number	Percentage
Biological science	32	11.2%
Business/management	45	15.7%
Education	14	4.9%
Engineering	35	12.2%
Humanities	63	22.1%
Journalism/communications	12	4.2%
Nursing	15	5.2%
Physical science/mathematics	17	5.9%
Social science	51	17.8%

Note. 322 respondents did not specify a disciplinary or department affiliation.

Table 3.2
Percentage of Total of Discipline- or Department–based Courses by Institution Type (N = 285)

	Institution Type	
Discipline Cluster	Public	Private
Biological science	12.5%	9.8%
Business/management	16.7%	14.7%
Education	4.9%	4.9%
Engineering	17.4%	7%
Humanities	18.1%	26%
Journalism/communications	5.5%	2.8%
Nursing	2.8%	7.7%
Physical science/math	4.2%	7.7%
Social science	16.7%	19%
Percentage of total	50.1%	49.8%

As noted in Table 3.2, engineering courses described in this survey were much more likely to be offered at public institutions than private institutions, these engineering courses are much more likely to be taught at institutions enrolling a total of 1,001 to 5,000 and more than 10,000 students than they are to be taught at institutions of other sizes (Table 3.3).

Social science courses represented in this survey are more likely to be taught at institutions with entire student populations of between 5,001 and 10,000, and nearly half of the total respondents who described discipline- and department-based courses indicated that these courses are taught at institutions enrolling between 1,001 and 5,000 students.

Table 3.3

Percentage of Total of Discipline- or Department-based Courses by Institution Enrollment Level (N = 285)

Discipline Cluster	Enrollment Level			
	1,000 and Under	1,001-5,000	5,001-10,000	Over 10,000
Biological science	8.5%	6.4%	11.1%	19.1%
Business/ management	11.4%	18.4%	19.4%	12.3%
Education	5.7%	4.8%	0	6.7%
Engineering	2.8%	15.2%	2.7%	15.7%
Humanities	40%	20.8%	16.6%	19.1%
Journalism/ communications	0	4.8%	2.7%	5.6%
Nursing	5.7%	6.4%	8.3%	2.2%
Physical science/math	2.8%	7.2%	5.5%	5.6%
Social science	22.8%	16%	33.3%	12.3%
Percentage of total	12.2%	43.8%	12.6%	31.2%

"...nearly half of the total respondents who described discipline- and department-based courses indicated that these courses are taught at institutions enrolling between 1,001 and 5,000 students."

Table 3.4

Percentage of Total of Discipline- or Department-based Courses by Institution Selectivity (N = 285)

Disciplinary Cluster	Selectivity		
	High	Medium	Low
Biological science	7.6%	11.9%	6.6%
Business/management	7.6%	15.7%	20%
Education	7.6%	5.3%	0
Engineering	15.3%	10.3%	26.6%
Humanities	30.7%	20.2%	33.3%
Journalism/communications	0	4.5%	3.3%
Nursing	0	6.2%	0
Physical science/math	0	7%	0
Social science	30.7%	18.1%	10%
Percentage of total	4.5%	84.9%	10.5%

Respondents who described social science courses in this survey are three times more likely to be from highly selective institutions than they are institutions of low selectivity, and respondents who described business and management courses are more than twice as likely to be from medium and low selectivity institutions than they are highly selective institutions (Table 3.4). Most of the respondents who described discipline- and department-based senior seminars and capstone courses in this survey are from institutions of medium selectivity. As noted above, a narrative analysis of responses by discipline cluster is provided in the final section of this chapter.

"Most of the respondents who described discipline- and department-based senior seminars and capstone courses in this survey are from institutions of medium selectivity."

1. Course Goals

According to the results of this survey, discipline- and department-based senior seminars and capstone courses, across disciplines, are intended to cap learning within the academic major (Tables 3.5 through 3.7). More than 60% of respondents indicated that this was the primary goal of these courses (Table 3.5). The second most frequently cited number one goal, promoting integration and connections between the academic major and work world, was slightly more likely to be listed by respondents from public institutions. Only 1.4% of respondents from public institutions and .91% of respondents from private institutions indicated that promoting the coherence and relevance of general education is a primary goal of these courses.

Table 3.5
Number One Goal of Discipline- or Department-based Courses by Institution Type (N = 607)

	Institution Type	
Goal	Public	Private
Fostering integration and synthesis within the academic major	63%	67%
Promoting integration and connections between the academic major and work world	16.4%	11.8%
Improving seniors' career preparation and pre-professional development	7.8%	5.4%
Promoting integration and connections between general education and the academic major	3.5%	4.5%
Promoting the coherence and relevance of general education	1.4%	.91%
Explicitly and intentionally developing important student skills, competencies, and perspectives which are tacitly or incidentally developed in the college curriculum (e.g., leadership skills)	3.2%	4.8%
Other	1%	2.7%
Promoting effective life planning and decision making with respect to issues that will be encountered in adult life after college	.36%	.61%
Enhancing seniors' preparation and prospects for postgraduate education	2.1%	2.7%
Enhancing awareness of and support for key personal adjustments encountered by seniors during their transition from college to post-college life	2.1%*	.30%

Note. Totals do not add to 100%. Some respondents selected more than one number one goal.

*p<.05

"Only 1.4% of respondents from public institutions and .91% of respondents from private institutions indicated that promoting the coherence and relevance of general education is a primary goal of these courses."

Table 3.6
Number One Goal of Discipline- or Department-based Courses by Institution Enrollment Level (N = 607)

Goal	Enrollment Level			
	1,000 and Under	1,001-5,000	5,001-10,000	Over 10,000
Fostering integration and synthesis within the academic major	65.2%	67.6%	68.8%	58.5%
Promoting integration and connections between the academic major and work world	11.5%	14.1%	10%	17.6%
Improving seniors' career preparation and pre-professional development	9.4%	4.3%	4.4%	10.2%
Promoting integration and connections between general education and the academic major	4.2%	4%	5.5%	3.4%
Promoting the coherence and relevance of general education	1%	.73%	2.2%	1.3%
Explicitly and intentionally developing important student skills, competencies, and perspectives which are tacitly or incidentally developed in the college curriculum (e.g., leadership skills)	5.2%	3.2%	4.4%	4.7%
Other	3.1%	2.5%	0	1.3%
Promoting effective life planning and decision making with respect to issues that will be encountered in adult life after college	1%	.36%	1.1%	0
Enhancing seniors' preparation and prospects for postgraduate education	6.3%	1.8%	2.2%	1.3%
Enhancing awareness of and support for key personal adjustments encountered by seniors during their transition from college to post-college life	1%	.73%	2.2%	1.3%

Note. Totals do not add to 100%. Some respondents selected more than one number one goal.

In terms of size of institution (Table 3.6), respondents from large institutions were more likely than respondents from institutions of other sizes to mark as a primary goal integrating the academic major and the world of work and improving seniors' preparation for work.

Respondents from the smallest institutions were more than twice as likely than respondents from institutions of other sizes to indicate that the courses they described focused on enhancing seniors' preparation and prospects for postgraduate education. As Table 3.7 indicates, respondents from highly selective institutions were much less likely than respondents from institutions of medium and low selectivity to mark as a goal of these discipline- and department-based courses promoting integration and connections between the academic major and work world.

Table 3.7

Number One Goal of Discipline- or Department-based Courses by Institution Selectivity (N = 607)

Goal	Selectivity		
	High	Medium	Low
Fostering integration and synthesis within the academic major	80%	65.2%	63.5%
Promoting integration and connections between the academic major and work world	3.6%	16.6%	14.7%
Improving seniors' career preparation and pre-professional development	9.4%	4.3%	4.4%
Promoting integration and connections between general education and the academic major	0	2.7%	4.7%
Promoting the coherence and relevance of general education	1.8%	0	1.2%
Explicitly and intentionally developing important student skills, competencies, and perspectives which are tacitly or incidentally developed in the college curriculum (e.g., leadership skills)	1.8%	5.5%	4.1%
Other	3.6%	1.3%	1.8%
Promoting effective life planning and decision making with respect to issues that will be encountered in adult life after college	0	0	.63%
Enhancing seniors' preparation and prospects for postgraduate education	1.8%	0	2.9%
Enhancing awareness of and support for key personal adjustments encountered by seniors during their transition from college to post-college life	0	1.39%	1.25%

Note. Totals do not add to 100%. Some respondents selected more than one number one goal.

Table 3.8
Instructional Responsibility for Discipline- or Department-based Courses by Institution Type (N= 607)

Instructional Staff	Exclusive Responsibility		As Part of a Team	
	Public	Private	Public	Private
Faculty	74.9%	71%	24%	28%
Career professionals	.72%	1.8%	1.4%	1.5%
Community leaders	1.7%*	.91%**	2.1%	3.6%
Other	1%	.3%	.3%	.3%
Other student affairs professionals	0	.3%	0	.3%
Graduate students	.36%	0	0	.3

Note. Totals do not add to 100%. Some sections of the same courses are taught by different individuals. Comparisons are between exclusive responsibility versus team approach across the same institution types.

*p<.05   **p<.01

2. Instructional Responsibility

Tables 3.8, 3.9, and 3.10 offer analyses of instructional responsibility by the three key variables. More than 70% of the respondents from public and private institutions indicated that these courses are taught by individual faculty members (Table 3.8).

"More than 70% of the respondents from public and private institutions indicated that these courses are taught by individual faculty members."

Other instructors, working alone or in teams, were identified by less than 4% of the respondents across institution types. In terms of institution size, there was a general tendency for respondents from larger institutions to indicate that community leaders participate in the instruction of these courses (Table 3.9).

Table 3.9

Instructional Responsibility for Discipline- or Department-based Courses by Institution Enrollment Level (N = 607)

Instructional Staff	Exclusive Responsibility				As Part of a Team			
	1,000 and Under	1,001-5,000	5,001-10,000	Over 10,000	1,000 and Under	1,001-5,000	5,001-10,000	Over 10,000
Faculty	69.4%	72%	76.6%	74.1%	29.4%	27.6%	23.3%	24.4%
Career professionals	1%	2.5%	0	0	1%	2.1%	1.1%	1.3%
Community leaders	1%	1%*	3.3%*	.68%**	1.0%	1.8%	4.4%	5.4%
Other	0	.36%	1.1%	1.3%	0	.73%	0	0
Other student affairs professionals	0	.36%	0	0	0	.36%	0	0
Graduate students	0	0	0	.68%	0	0	0	.68

Note. Totals do not add to 100%. Some sections of the same courses are taught by different individuals. Comparisons are between exclusive responsibility versus team approach across institutions of the same enrollment levels.

*$p<.05$ **$p<.01$

"*In terms of institution size, there was a general tendency for respondents from larger institutions to indicate that community leaders participate in the instruction of these courses.*"

Table 3.10

Instructional Responsibility for Discipline- or Department-based Courses by Institution Selectivity (N = 607)

Instructional Staff	Exclusive Responsibility			As Part of a Team		
	High	Medium	Low	High	Medium	Low
Faculty	56.3%	74.7%	72.2%	43.6%	24.3%	27.7%
Career professionals	0	1.2%	2.7%	1.8%	1.2%	2.7%
Community leaders	1.8%	1.4%**	0*	5.4%	2.7%	2.7%
Other	0	.83%	0	0	.21%	0
Other student affairs professionals	0	.21%	0	0	0	1.3%
Graduate students	0	.21%	0	0	.21%	0

Note. Totals do not add to 100%. Some sections of the same courses are taught by different individuals. Comparisons are between exclusive responsibility versus team approach across institutions of the same selectivity levels.

*p<.05   **p<.01

The most notable difference is between institutions of different selectivity levels. Although respondents indicated that instructors other than faculty members are rarely involved in discipline- and department-based senior seminars and capstone courses, respondents from highly selective institutions did suggest that faculty members teaching these courses are almost equally likely to work in teams as they are to teach these courses alone (Table 3.10).

"...respondents from highly selective institutions did suggest that faculty members teaching these courses are almost equally likely to work in teams as they are to teach these courses alone."

3. Course Enrollment Levels

Most sections of discipline- and department-based senior seminars and capstone courses, across institution types, institution enrollment and selectivity levels, are reported in this survey to enroll 30 or fewer students (Tables 3.11, 3.12, and 3.13). There is reported to be little difference between sizes of these sections at public and private institutions (Table 3.11).

Table 3.11

Maximum Section Enrollments of Discipline- or Department-based Courses by Institution Type (N = 607)

Enrollment Range	Institution Type	
	Public	Private
0-9	9.2%	11.2%
10-19	10.8%	18.1%
20-29	15.8%	17.3%
30-39	6.4%	4.9%
40-49	1.9%	.9%
50-75	1.1%	.9%
76-99	0	.1%
100+	.3%	.3%
Total Percentage	45.9%	54%

"Most sections of discipline- and department-based senior seminars and capstone courses, across institution types, institution enrollment and selectivity levels, are reported in this survey to enroll 30 or fewer students."

Table 3.12
Maximum Section Enrollments in Discipline- or Department-based Courses by Institution Enrollment Level (N = 607)

	Enrollment Level			
Enrollment Range	1,000 and Under	1,001-5,000	5,001-10,000	Over 10,000
0-9	21%	18.9%	17.7%	24.4%
10-19	33.6%	34.9%	24.4%	17.6%
20-29	30.5%	33.4%	41.1%	29.2%
30-39	8.4%	9%	11.1%	17.6%
40-49	4.2%	1%	4.4%	4.7%
50-75	1%	2.5%	1.1%	3.4%
76-99	1%	0	0	0
100+	0	0	0	2.7%

$p < .01$

Responses indicate that size of institution and section size slightly increase together (Table 3.12), and courses at institutions of medium selectivity are reported in this survey to be slightly larger than those at institutions of either high or low selectivity (Table 3.13).

"Responses indicate that size of institution and section size slightly increase together..."

Table 3.13

Maximum Section Enrollments in Discipline- or Department-based Courses by Institution Selectivity (N = 607)

Enrollment Range	Selectivity		
	High	Medium	Low
0-9	23.6%	20.6%	16.6%
10-19	29%	28.5%	31.9%
20-29	32.7%	32.9%	34.7%
30-39	10.9%	11.4%	11.1%
40-49	1.8%	2.9%	4.1%
50-75	1.8%	2.5%	1.3%
76-99	0	.2%	0
100+	0	.8%	0
Percentage of Total	9%	79%	11.8%

Table 3.14
Amount of Credit Granted by Discipline- or Department-based Courses by Institution Type (N = 567)

	Institution Type	
Credit Hours	Public	Private
One qtr.	0	.3%
Two qtrs.	.3%	.9%
Three qtrs.	.3%	.9%
Four qtrs.	.7%	1.6%
Five qtrs.	1.8%	0
Six or more qtrs.	1.1%	.6%
One sem.	5.6%	7.2%
Two sems.	3.4%	6.9%
Three sems.	69.7%	54.7%
Four or more sems.	16.6%	26.4%

p<.01

4. Amount and Type of Academic Credit and Grading Practices

According to respondents to this survey, discipline- and department-based senior seminars and capstone courses at private institutions are more likely to carry four or more semester credits than courses at public institutions, although the majority of these courses at both types of institutions reportedly are offered for three semester credits (Table 3.14).

Little difference was reported to exist across courses at institutions of different enrollment levels (Table 3.15). However, institutional selectivity level does appear to make some difference in the amount of credit these courses carry (Table 3.16).

Table 3.15
Amount of Credit Granted by Discipline- or Department-based Courses by Institution Enrollment Level (N = 567)

Credits Hours	Enrollment Level			
	1,000 and Under	1,001-5,000	5,001-10,000	Over 10,000
One qtr.	1.1%	0	0	0
Two qtrs.	1.1%	.7%	1.1%	0
Three qtrs.	1.1%	.7%	1.1%	0
Four qtrs.	1.1%	1.5%	0	1.4%
Five qtrs.	0	.7%	1.1%	1.4%
Six or more qtrs.	0	.3%	0	2.8%
One sem.	3.4%	7.8%	9.3%	4.3%
Two sems.	5.6%	4.7%	3.4%	7.1%
Three sems.	68.1%	55.5%	72%	62.5%
Four or more sems.	18.1%	27.5%	11.6%	20.1%

"...institutional selectivity level does appear to make some difference in the amount of credit these courses carry."

Table 3.16
*Amount of Credit Granted by Discipline- or Department-based
Courses by Institution Selectivity (N = 567)*

Credit Hours	Selectivity		
	High	Medium	Low
One qtr.	0	0	1.4%
Two qtrs.	2%	.67%	0
Three qtrs.	0	.67%	1.4%
Four qtrs.	4.1%	.67%	2.9%
Five qtrs.	2%	.67%	1.4%
Six or more qtrs.	2%	.89%	0
One sem.	14.5%	6.2%	2.9%
Two sems.	0	5.3%	8.8%
Three sems.	41.6%	63.4%	64.7%
Four or more sems.	33.3%	21.5%	16.1%

p<.01

As selectivity increased, the likelihood increased that the respondents would indicate that these courses are offered for either one or four semester credits. As selectivity decreased, the likelihood increased that the respondents would indicate that these courses are offered for two or three semester credits.

Tables 3.17, 3.18, and 3.19 report findings on the type of credit granted by discipline- and department-based senior seminars and capstone courses. Again, type of institution (Table 3.17) and institution enrollment level (Table 3.18), are reportedly not as important as institution selectivity level (Table 3.19).

Table 3.17

Type of Credit Granted by Discipline- or Department-based Courses by Institution Type (N = 607)

Granting Credit	Institution Type	
	Public	Private
Yes	97.1%	98.1%
No	2.8%	1.8%

Type of Grade	Institution Type	
	Public	Private
Pass/fail	6.4%	5.1%
Letter grade	93.5%	94.8%

Credit Applied As	Institution Type	
	Public	Private
Core requirement	19.7%	16.1%
Elective	2.5%	1.8%
Major requirement	74.5%	79.2%
General education requirement	1.7%	1.2%
Other	1.4%	1.5%

Table 3.18
Type of Credit Granted by Discipline- or Department-based Courses
by Institution Enrollment Level (N = 607)

| | Enrollment Level | | | |
Granting Credit	1,000 and Under	1,001-5,000	5,001-10,000	Over 10,000
Yes	100%	97.4%	95.5%	97.9%
No	0	2.5%	4.4%	2%

| | Enrollment Level | | | |
Type of Grade	1,000 and Under	1,001-5,000	5,001-10,000	Over 10,000
Pass/fail	5.2%	5%	7.7%	6.1%
Letter grade	94.7%	94.9%	92.2%	93.8%

| | Enrollment Level | | | |
Credit Applied As	1,000 and Under	1,001-5,000	5,001-10,000	Over 10,000
Core requirement	16.8%	15.6%	18.8%	21.7%
Elective	1%	1%	1.1%	5.4%
Major requirement	80%	80.7%	74.4%	70%
General education requirement	1%	1.8%	3.3%	0
Other	1%	.73%	2.2%	2.7%

$p<.05$

Responses from highly selective institutions indicate that these courses are less likely to carry academic credit and more likely to be graded pass/fail than courses at institutions of medium or low selectivity levels.

Table 3.19

Type of Credit Granted by Discipline- or Department-based Courses by Institution Selectivity (N = 607)

	Selectivity		
Granting Credit	High	Medium	Low
Yes	92.7%	98.1%	98.6%
No	7.2%	1.8%	1.3%

$p<.05$

	Selectivity		
Type of Grade	High	Medium	Low
Pass/fail	7.2%	1.3%	6.2%
Letter grade	92.7%	98.6%	93.7%

	Selectivity		
Credit Applied As	High	Medium	Low
Core requirement	10.9%	18.3%	19.4%
Elective	5.4%	1.8%	1.3%
Major requirement	78.1%	76.8%	77.7%
General education requirement	1.8%	1.4%	1.3%
Other	3.6%	1.4%	0

$p<.01$

Table 3.20
Length of Discipline- or Department-based Courses by Institution Type (N = 585)

	Institution Type	
Length of Courses	Public	Private
1-8 weeks	.37%	1.5%
1 quarter	2.9%	3.1%
1 semester	89.3%	82.4%
2 quarters	1.4%	.96%
2 semesters	5.9%	11.7%

Table 3.21
Length of Discipline- or Department-based Courses by Institution Enrollment Level (N = 585)

	Enrollment Level			
Length of Course	1,000 and Under	1,001-5,000	5,001-10,000	Over 10,000
1-8 weeks	1.1%	1.1%	0	1.4%
1 quarter	0	3.7%	3.4%	3.5%
1 semester	86.6%	86.8%	88.6%	80.8%
2 quarters	1.1%	.38%	1.1%	2.8%
2 semesters	11.1%	7.8%	6.8%	11.3%

5. Length of Course

Regarding the duration of discipline- and department-based courses, respondents from private institutions were twice as likely to indicate that these courses are offered for two semesters than respondents from public institutions (Table 3.20), although more than 80% of respondents from both types of institutions noted that these courses are held for just one semester. There is reported to be little difference in the length of these courses across institutional enrollment levels (Table 3.21).

Selectivity level does appear to make some difference, with respondents from highly selective institutions twice as likely than respondents from institutions of other selectivity levels to report that these courses are offered for two semesters (Table 3.22).

6. Administrative Responsibility

With few exceptions, all respondents describing discipline- and department-based senior seminars reported that these courses are administered through individual academic departments.

Table 3.22
Length of Discipline- or Department-based Courses by Institution Selectivity (N = 585)

Length of Course	Selectivity		
	High	Medium	Low
1-8 weeks	0	1%	1.4%
1 quarter	6%	2.8%	2.8%
1 semester	70%	86.8%	88.5%
2 quarters	8%	.65%	0
2 semesters	16%	8.6%	7.1%

"…respondents from highly selective institutions [were] twice as likely than respondents from institutions of other selectivity levels to report that these courses are offered for two semesters."

Table 3.23
Instructional Components of Discipline- or Department-based Courses by Institution Type (N = 607)

Instructional Component	Frequency of Use by Institution Type	
	Public	Private
Oral presentation	79.2%	79.8%
Major project	80.2%	79.2%
Group project	57.3%**	43.6%
Final exam	47.6%*	38.1%
Portfolio development	42.6%	35.3%
Thesis	21.8%**	38.7%
Use of career center	16.8%*	10.3%
Internship	12.5%*	20.1%
Other	11.4%	13.7%
Explicit consideration of graduate school	13.6%	14%
Alumni involvement/networking	13.9%	10%
Leadership training	12.9%	9.7%
Service learning/community service	10%	8.8%
Educational travel	3.2%	5.4%
Employment (remunerative/non-remunerative)	1.4%	3.9%
Work shadowing	2.5%	3%

Note. Totals do not add to 100%. Respondents were asked to check all that apply.

*$p<.05$ **$p<.01$

7. Instructional Practices

According to these survey results, discipline- and department-based senior seminars and capstone courses at public institutions are more likely than courses at private institutions to incorporate group projects, final examinations, and use of career centers (Table 3.23). Responses indicate that courses at private institutions are more likely than courses at public institutions to require thesis writing and completion of internships. Across both types of institutions, oral presentations and major projects were the most likely to be marked by respondents. These survey responses indicate that courses at the smallest institutions are more likely than courses at larger institutions to require thesis writing.

Explicit consideration of graduate school is reportedly twice as likely to be a component of courses at small institutions than it is at large institutions (Table 3.24). Conversely, leadership training and educational travel were more likely to be marked by respondents at the largest institutions than they were to be marked by respondents from the smallest institutions.

Table 3.24

Instructional Components of Discipline- or Department-based Courses by Institution Enrollment Level (N = 607)

Instructional Component	Frequency of Use by Enrollment Level			
	1,000 and Under	1,001-5,000	5,001-10,000	Over 10,000
Oral presentation	86.3%	80.3%	78.8%	74.1%
Major project	77.8%	80.3%	77.7%	80.9%
Group project	40%	49%	52.2%	56.4%
Final exam	44.2%	40.3%	43.3%	44.9%
Portfolio development	38.9%	40.7%	41.1%	33.3%
Thesis	37.8%**	36.3%	22.2%	21.7%
Use of career center	9.4%	13.8%	15.5%	13.6%
Internship	21%	17.4%	15.5%	12.9%
Other	16.8%	10.1%	16.6%	12.2%
Explicit consideration of graduate school	21%	12.7%	16.6%	9.5%
Alumni involvement/ networking	8.4%	10.5%	11.1%	17%
Leadership training	9.4%	9%	11.1%	16.3%
Service learning/ community service	10.5%	9%	10%	8.8%
Educational travel	2.1%	4.3%	3.3%	6.8%
Employment (remunerative/ non-remunerative)	4.2%	3.2%	1.1%	2%
Work shadowing	4.2%	1.8%	4.4%	2.7%

Note. Totals do not add to 100%. Respondents were asked to check all that apply.

**$p<.01$

Table 3.25
Instructional Components of Discipline- or Department-based Courses by Institution Selectivity (N = 607)

Instructional Component	Frequency of Use by Selectivity		
	High	Medium	Low
Oral presentation	78.1%	79.5%	80.5%
Major project	78.1%	79.7%	80.5%
Group project	38.1%	51.8%	45.8%
Final exam	34.5%	43.5%	41.6%
Portfolio development	30.9%	39.7%	37.5%
Thesis	50.9%**	20.8%	30.2%
Use of career center	5.4%	14.5%	11.1%
Internship	7.2%	17.9%	15.2%
Other	9%	14.1%	5.5%
Explicit consideration of graduate school	10.9%	15.4%	5.5%
Alumni involvement/networking	5.4%*	13.7%	4.1%
Leadership training	7.2%	11.2%	13.8%
Service learning/community service	5.4%	9.7%	9.7%
Educational travel	0	5%	4.1%
Employment (remunerative/non-remunerative)	1.8%	2.7%	4.1%
Work shadowing	1.8%	2.5%	5.5%

Note. Totals do not add to 100%. Respondents were asked to check all that apply.

*p<.05   **p<.01

Thesis writing was also the component most differentiating courses at institutions of various selectivity levels (Table 3.25). Respondents from medium selectivity institutions were more likely to indicate that courses there incorporate use of career centers, internships, and alumni involvement or networking. Leadership training and work shadowing distinguished the responses from institutions of low selectivity. Across all three key variables, service learning was indicated by 10% or fewer of these respondents to be a component of discipline- or department-based senior seminars and capstone courses. Other instructional components written in by survey respondents included major papers, fine arts performances, exhibitions, standardized tests, the design and building of a prototype, clinical experience, and preparation for examinations and interviews. A few respondents also indicated that these courses are co-requisites with internships and student teaching.

8. Populations Required to Take the Course

More than 70% of respondents from both public and private institutions indicated that the courses they described are required (Table 3.26). The same percentage of respondents from institutions of all enrollment levels also indicated that these courses are required, except for courses at institutions with total enrollments of over 10,000 students (Table 3.27). Just over 64% of these respondents indicated that these courses are required for all students. According to these survey responses, discipline- and department-based senior seminars and capstone courses at highly selective institutions are less likely to be required for all students than courses at institutions of medium and low selectivity.

Table 3.26
Students Required to Take Discipline- or Department-based Courses by Institution Type (N = 607)

Students Required to Take Course	Institution Type	
	Public	Private
All	70.2%	71.3%
Some	27.9%	28%
None	1.7%	.61%

Table 3.27
Students Required to Take Discipline- or Department-based Courses by Institution Enrollment Level (N = 607)

Students Required to Take Course	Enrollment Level			
	1,000 and Under	1,001-5,000	5,001-10,000	Over 10,000
All	71.5%	73.4%	72.2%	64.6%
Some	28.4%	26.1%	25.5%	32.6%
None	0	.36%	2.2%	2.7%

"More than 70% of respondents from both public and private institutions indicated that the courses they described are required."

Table 3.28
Students Required to Take Discipline- or Department-based Courses by Institution Selectivity (N = 607)

	Selectivity		
Students Required to Take Course	High	Medium	Low
All	58.1%	72%	72.2%
Some	38.1%	26.8%	27.7%
None	3.6%	1%	0

Table 3.29
Gender Ratio of Discipline- or Department-based Courses by Institution Type (N = 67)

	Institution Type	
Gender Ratio	Public	Private
70% women	16.1%	16.6%
50 – 70% women	32.2%	30.5%
50/50	9.6%	33.3%
50 – 70% men	25.8%	13.8%
70% men	16.1%	5.5%

Note. Applies only to elective courses.

Close to 60% of respondents from highly selective institutions indicated that these courses are required for all students (Table 3.28). That number is over 70% for respondents at both medium and low selectivity institutions. Respondents indicated that when these courses are offered as electives at both public and private institutions they are more often subscribed to by women than men (Table 3.29).

Responses indicate a general tendency for males to enroll in elective discipline- and department-based courses at a higher rate as the size of the institution increases (Table 3.30). Forty percent of respondents from highly selective institutions noted that the elective courses they described enrolled 70% males, while that number was 0 for institutions of low selectivity (Table 3.31).

Table 3.30
Gender Ratio of Discipline- or Department-based Courses by Institution Enrollment Level (N = 67)

	Enrollment Level			
Gender Ratio	1,000 and Under	1,001-5,000	5,001-10,000	Over 10,000
70% women	23%	16.1%	20%	7.6%
50 – 70% women	30.7%	29%	30%	38.4%
50/50	38.4%	16.1%	30%	15.3%
50 – 70% men	7.6%	29%	10%	15.3%
70% men	0	9.6%	10%	23%

Note. Applies only to elective courses.

Table 3.31
Gender Ratio of Discipline- or Department-based Courses by Institution Selectivity (N = 67)

	Selectivity		
Gender Ratio	High	Medium	Low
70% women	0	20%	8.3%
50 – 70% women	0	34%	33.3%
50/50	60%	24%	0
50 – 70% men	0	12%	58.3%
70% men	40%	10%	0

Note. Applies only to elective courses.

Table 3.32

Length of Existence at Institution of Discipline- or Department-based Courses by Institution Type (N = 480)

	Institution Type	
Range of Years	Public	Private
< 1	0	.7%
1-5	32.2%	34.2%
6-10	25.4%	23.4%
11-15	15%	12.3%
16-20	12.7%	12.6%
21-25	7.7%	5%
26-30	4%	6.9%
31-35	1.3%	1.5%
36-40	0	1.5%
41-45	0	.3%
46-50	.4%	.3%
51-78	.9%	.7%

9. Length of Existence at the Institution

According to this survey, discipline- and department-based senior seminars and capstone courses at private institutions are reported to be slightly older than their counterparts at public institutions. Respondents indicated that more courses at private institutions have existed for 26 or more years. More than half of the courses at both types of institutions are reported to be between one and 10 years old (Table 3.32).

"...discipline- and department-based senior seminars and capstone courses at private institutions are reported to be slightly older than their counterparts at public institutions."

This holds true across courses from institutions of various enrollment levels (Table 3.33). A positive correlation exists between age of courses and selectivity of institution (Table 3.34). Responses indicate that courses at highly selective institutions have existed longer than those at institutions of medium selectivity and that courses at low selectivity institutions have not existed as long as those at institutions of medium selectivity.

Table 3.33

Length of Existence at Institution of Discipline- or Department-based Courses by Institution Enrollment Level (N = 480)

Range of Years	Enrollment Level			
	1,000 and Under	1,001-5,000	5,001-10,000	Over 10,000
< 1	0	.9%	0	0
1-5	28.4%	36.7%	30.1%	32.4%
6-10	25.9%	23.7%	21.9%	26.1%
11-15	11.1%	12.5%	20.5%	12.6%
16-20	13.5%	11.6%	15%	12.6%
21-25	9.8%	5.5%	8.2%	3.6%
26-30	6.1%	4.6%	2.7%	9%
31-35	1.2%	1.4%	1.3%	1.8%
36-40	2.4%	.9%	0	0
41-45	0	.4%	0	0
46-50	1.2%	0	0	.9%
51-78	0	1.4%	0	.9%

Table 3.34
Length of Existence at Institution of Discipline- or Department-based Courses by Institution Selectivity (N = 480)

| | Selectivity | | |
Range of Years	High	Medium	Low
< 1	0	.5%	0
1-5	25%	32.3%	45.6%
6-10	22.2%	24.5%	24.5%
11-15	11.1%	14.7%	7%
16-20	13.8%	12.4%	14.4%
21-25	11.1%	5.6%	7%
26-30	8.3%	5.9%	1.7%
31-35	5.5%	1.2%	0
36-40	2.7%	.7%	0
41-45	0	.2%	0
46-50	0	.5%	0
51-78	0	1%	0

Table 3.35
Evaluation of Discipline- or Department-based Courses by Institution Type (N = 607)

| | Institution Type | |
Course Evaluated	Public	Private
Yes	77.7%	80.4%

10. Evaluation Practices

This survey indicates that discipline- and department-based senior seminars and capstone courses at public institutions are slightly less likely than courses at private institutions to be evaluated (Table 3.35) and courses at the largest institutions are slightly less likely to be evaluated than those at the smallest institutions (Table 3.36).

Responses suggest that courses at institutions of low selectivity are less likely to be evaluated than courses at institutions of high selectivity (Tables 3.37) Overall, percentages range from a low of 73.6% of respondents at low selectivity institutions who indicated that these courses are evaluated to a high of 84.2% of respondents from institutions with total student enrollments of under 1,000 who indicated the same. Respondents reported that students and faculty participating in these courses conduct these evaluations.

Table 3.36
Evaluation of Discipline- or Department-based Courses by Institution Enrollment Level (N = 607)

	Enrollment Level			
Course Evaluated	1,000 and Under	1,001-5,000	5,001-10,000	Over 10,000
Yes	84.2%	78.1%	83.3%	75.5%

Table 3.37
Evaluation of Discipline- or Department-based Courses by Institution Selectivity (N = 607)

	Selectivity		
Course Evaluated	High	Medium	Low
Yes	81.8%	79.7%	73.6%

$p<.05$

"...courses at institutions of low selectivity are less likely to be evaluated than courses at institutions of high selectivity."

Table 3.38
Assessment Tied to Discipline- or Department-based Courses by Institution Type (N = 607)

Course Tied to Comprehensive Assessment	Institution Type	
	Public	Private
Yes	40.1%	49%

p<.05

Table 3.39
Assessment Tied to Discipline- or Department-based Courses by Institution Enrollment Level (N = 607)

Course Tied to Comprehensive Assessment	Institution Type			
	1,000 and Under	1,001-5,000	5,001-10,000	Over 10,000
Yes	65.2%	40.3%	38.8%	29.2%

p<.01

Table 3.40
Assessment Tied to Discipline- or Department-based Courses by Institution Enrollment Level (N = 864)

Course Tied to Comprehensive Assessment	Selectivity		
	High	Medium	Low
Yes	40%	43%	58%

p<.01

11. Assessment Practices

Less than half of the respondents to this survey indicated that discipline- and department-based senior seminars and capstone courses they described are involved in comprehensive assessment. By institution type, it was reported that courses at private institutions are less likely to be involved in such a process than courses at public institutions (Table 3.38). Responses indicate that there is a negative correlation between ties to comprehensive assessment and size of institution, with courses at the smallest institutions reported to be the most likely to be involved in such an assessment process (Table 3.39). A negative correlation was reported between selectivity of institution and likelihood of involvement in assessment, with responses indicating that courses at highly selective institutions are the least likely to be involved in a comprehensive assessment process.

Summary of Analysis – Discipline- and Department-based Courses

This survey indicates that selectivity level of an institution, over institution type and enrollment level, is the variable that determines the greatest difference in discipline- and department-based senior seminars and capstone courses. For example, highly selective institutions were less likely to be reported to offer business and engineering courses and more likely to report offering social science courses. Differences between types of courses at other types and sizes of institutions were not as great. Respondents at highly selective institutions were less likely to report that the goals of these courses are to prepare students for the world of work. Respondents at highly selective institutions noted that faculty members are much more likely to work in teams than faculty members from institutions of other selectivity levels. Private and highly selective institutions, the respondents reported, are more likely than other institutions to offer discipline- and department-based senior seminars and capstone courses for two or more semesters. Highly selective institutions are more likely than other institutions, according to this survey, to require thesis writing in senior seminars and capstone courses based in the discipline or department and less likely to require use of career centers, internships, alumni involvement and networking, leadership training and work shadowing.

These courses at highly selective institutions are reportedly less likely than courses at other institutions to be required and more of these type of courses are reported to be graded pass/fail. The courses described in this survey from highly selective institutions are older than those from other institutions and are evaluated more often than courses at institutions of other selectivity levels. Responses indicate that discipline- and department-based senior seminars and capstone courses at highly selective institutions are not involved in comprehensive assessment efforts as often courses at other institutions. In sum, the selectivity of an institution seems to matter most when examining the practices and processes of discipline- and department-based senior seminars and capstone courses represented in this survey.

Two striking similarities in these courses across all three key variables are a consistent lack of interest in incorporating service learning, experiences that link community service with in-class activities and assignments, into these courses, and a nearly universal disinterest in promoting the coherence and relevance of general education.

Summary of Findings by Discipline Cluster

Of the 285 respondents reporting on discipline- or department-based courses, the single greatest number (63) described humanities courses and the smallest number (12) offered information on journalism and communications courses. A summary of the analysis for courses in each of the nine disciplinary clusters is offered below, followed by a summary of analysis for courses in all nine clusters together.

Biological Sciences

A total of 32 respondents reported on courses in the biological sciences, slightly more than half of these are from public institutions. Ninety percent of the respondents indicated that the courses they were describing are offered at medium selectivity institutions and 90% said the courses are from institutions with 1,001 or more students. More than 50% of the respondents said the primary goals of the courses are to foster integration and synthesis within the academic major. The next two most frequently cited number one goals concerned integration between the academic world and the world of work, and enhancing awareness of key personal adjustment issues. Only one respondent each said that promoting the coherence and relevance of general education or integrating and connecting the academic major and general education are of primary importance in the courses described. Close to 70% of the respondents said the courses are taught by faculty members working alone and more than 90% indicated that sections of the courses enroll fewer than 30 students. More than 90% of the respondents said letter grades are assigned in the courses they described and 100% indicated that these courses are offered for credit. Most of the respondents indicated that the courses are offered for one to three credits, 75% noted that the courses described are designated requirements for the academic major, and nearly 90% of respondents said the courses are offered for one semester.

"Only one respondent each said that promoting the coherence and relevance of general education or integrating and connecting the academic major and general education are of primary importance in the courses described."

The most frequently indicated instructional technique was the oral presentation (80.6% of respondents said this is the number one approach used in the courses they described), followed by the major project, group project, and final examination. Fewer than 10% of respondents describing biological science courses in this sample included any activities or assignments involving on-the-job experience, service learning, educational travel, consideration of graduate school, or leadership training. Slightly more than 75% of respondents indicated that the courses are required for all students and they noted that most of these courses have been offered on their campuses for up to 15 years. Nearly 90% of respondents said these courses are evaluated, most by students in the courses and 25% indicated that these courses are incorporated into comprehensive assessment.

Business and Management

A total of 45 respondents reported on courses in business and management, slightly more than half of these are from public institutions. Nearly 90% of the respondents are from medium selectivity institutions and slightly more than half are from institutions enrolling between 1,001 and 5,000 students. More than 70% of the respondents said the primary goal of the courses described is fostering integration and synthesis within the academic major. The next most frequently cited number one goal concerned integration between the academic world and world of work. Only one respondent said promoting the coherence and relevance of general education is of primary importance, with two respondents indicating that integrating general education and academic major is most important in the courses they described.

"More than 90% of the respondents indicated that business and management courses is taught by faculty members working alone, the highest number of lone faculty instructors among discipline- or department-based courses."

More than 90% of the respondents indicated that business and management courses is taught by faculty members working alone, the highest number of lone faculty instructors among discipline- or department-based courses. According to these survey results, these courses are generally larger than those in other disciplines, with more than 50% of respondents indicating that sections of the courses they described enroll 30 or more students. All of the business and management courses reported on in the survey assign letter grades and nearly all grant credit for these courses, with most granting three credits. Respondents indicated that these courses are treated as major requirements, and close to 90% of respondents said the courses they described are offered for one semester.

According to this survey, the most popular instructional technique in business and management courses is the major project (84.4% of respondents said this technique is used in the courses they were describing), followed by oral presentation, group project, and final examination. Fewer than 10% of respondents said these courses include any activities or assignments involving on-the-job experience, service learning, educational travel, or consideration of graduate school. In a departure from respondents representing other disciplines, close to 25% of respondents indicated that business and management courses include leadership training. More than 80% of respondents said the courses they described are required for all students and these courses are up to 20 years old. Just over 80% of respondents indicated that these courses are evaluated, most by students in the courses, and 40% said these courses are included in comprehensive assessment.

Education

Only 14 respondents reported on education courses, split evenly between responses on courses at public and private institutions. Respondents from medium selectivity institutions and those from institutions with enrollments over 1,001 students made up the majority of the respondents in this group. The most frequently cited number one goal of these courses is not that of other disciplines. Rather, it is integrating and connecting the academic major and world of work.

Integrating and synthesizing within the academic major and improving students' career preparation, the next most frequently cited number one goals, were half as likely to be marked by these respondents. Only one respondent indicated that general education, as it related to the academic major, is chiefly important in the course described. Just over half of the respondents reported that these courses are taught by faculty members working alone, the lowest number of solo instructors among all discipline- or department-based courses. More than 70% of respondents said sections of the courses enroll fewer than 30 students and just over 70% of respondents indicated that the courses carry a letter grade. All respondents noted that the courses they described grant credit, with most, as is typical of discipline- or department-based courses, granting three academic credits. According to survey respondents, these courses are treated as major requirements, and close to 90% of respondents indicated that these courses are offered for one semester.

"The most frequently cited number one goal of these courses is not that of other disciplines, rather, it is integrating and connecting the academic major and world of work."

In a departure from the instructional practices of other disciplines, education courses, as reported by these respondents, employ portfolio development as the pedagogical technique of choice. Oral presentations, use of the career center, group projects, and internships follow. According to these respondents, the instructional techniques least likely to be used are a required thesis, work shadowing, employment, and educational travel. Few education courses are reported to employ service learning or a final examination. Close to 80% of respondents indicated that the courses they described are required for all students and most of these courses are up to 15 years old. Just over 90% of the respondents indicated that the courses are evaluated, most by students in the courses, and about 30% of respondents reported that education senior seminars and capstone courses are included in comprehensive assessments.

Engineering

Most of the 35 respondents reporting on engineering courses are from public, medium selectivity institutions of more than 1,001 students. According to the results of this survey, engineering courses are the most singularly focused on the academic major and work preparation. The most frequently cited number one goal of these courses is integrating and synthesizing within the academic major, followed closely by integrating and connecting the academic major and world of work. Four respondents indicated career preparation as a number one goal of the courses, and one respondent indicated that promoting coherence and relevance of general education was most important in the course described. No other goal among the list of 10 choices was reported as a number one priority for these courses. Just over 60% of respondents indicated that these courses are taught by faculty members working alone, more than 70% of respondents said the courses enroll fewer than 30 students. All respondents said engineering courses carry letter grades. These courses are treated as a major requirement, and close to 40% of respondents said these courses are offered for four credits, a higher number than other discipline- or department-based courses. Respondents reported that credit for engineering senior seminars and capstone courses is treated as a major requirement, and 65% of respondents said these courses are offered for one semester.

"According to the results of this survey, engineering courses are the most singularly focused on the academic major and work preparation."

Major projects are reported to be required in nearly all of these courses, as are group projects, and, to a slightly lesser extent, oral presentations. The least likely instructional techniques to be marked by respondents include a required thesis, any assignment concerned with the work place, service learning, educational travel, and consideration of graduate school. More than 90% of respondents said the courses are required for all students and these courses have generally been offered for longer than courses in other disciplines, with 80% being up to 20 years old. Close to 80% of these courses are evaluated, most by students in the courses, and just over 35% are included in comprehensive assessment.

Humanities

More than half of the 63 respondents reporting on humanities courses represent private institutions (a greater number than courses in other disciplines), most of these from institutions of medium selectivity. More than 60% of the respondents are from institutions of fewer than 5,000 students. Nearly 70% of the respondents cited integrating and synthesizing within the academic major as the number one goal of the humanities courses described in the survey. Improving seniors' career preparation and pre-professional development was the next most frequently cited primary goal of humanities courses, at slightly more than 16%. Only four respondents selected integrating general education and the academic major as a number one goal of these courses and, according to these results, none of these humanities courses hold as a number one goal promoting the coherence and relevance of general education. Nearly 70% of the respondents indicated that these courses are taught by faculty members working alone. Nearly 90% of respondents indicated that each section of these courses enroll fewer than 30 students. Nearly all of these courses are reported to carry letter grades for these courses and all grant academic credit. Most grant three credits for these courses and most are treated as a major requirement. Nearly 90% of respondents indicated that these courses are offered for one semester.

"...none of these humanities courses hold as a number one goal promoting the coherence and relevance of general education."

Nearly 80% of respondents reported that major projects are the most frequently employed instructional technique in these humanities courses, with oral presentations following closely behind. Final examination is a third choice and portfolio development appeared in the top four instructional techniques used in humanities courses, a departure from all other disciplines except education, journalism/communications, and nursing. Slightly under 70% of respondents indicated that these courses are required for all students and most of these courses have been offered on their campuses for fewer than 15 years. Eighty percent of respondents indicated that these courses are evaluated, most by students in the courses, and just over 50% of respondents noted that these courses are included in comprehensive assessment.

Journalism and Communications

Only 12 courses were listed as either offered by journalism or communications departments, most from public institutions of medium selectivity. None were from the smallest sized institutions. Of this small sample, more than half of respondents indicated that the primary intent in these courses is to integrate and synthesize learning within the academic major. Promoting integration and connections between the academic major and work world was the second most frequently listed number one goal. Respondents indicated that none of these courses review general education, as a subject alone or as it relates to the academic major. Close to 85% of respondents indicated that these courses are taught by faculty members working alone, and close to that same percentage indicated that sections of these courses enroll fewer than 30 students. Respondents indicated that all of these courses grant letter grades, all grant academic

"Respondents [describing Journalism and Communications courses] indicated that none of these courses review general education, as a subject alone or as it relates to the academic major..."

credit, and nearly all are treated as a major requirement. More than 90% of respondents indicated that these courses are offered for one semester.

According to results of this survey, journalism and communications senior seminars and capstone courses require their students to complete a major project. The second most frequently cited instructional technique is portfolio development, followed by group project, and oral presentation. Slightly under 70% of the respondents indicated that these courses are required for all students and, according to these responses, these courses have been offered for less time than courses in other disciplines, with most being under 10 years old. Under 70% of respondents reported that these courses are evaluated, most by students in the courses, and just over 40% of respondents indicated that these courses are included in comprehensive assessment.

Nursing

The survey included responses from 15 individuals reporting on nursing courses, most from private institutions, all of medium selectivity and representing a broad range of institution sizes. Consistent with courses in other disciplines, nursing courses are reported to focus on the academic major and preparation for the world of work. Three of the courses each are reported to primarily attend to personal adjustment issues and developing student skills. Only one respondent reported that general education is a primary focus. A greater number of nursing courses than those in other disciplines except one are reported to be taught by instructional teams. Fifty three percent of respondents indicated that these courses are taught by faculty working alone, the second lowest (behind education courses) number of faculty working alone. Most of the course sections are held to enrollments under 30 students, only 66% of respondents indicated that the courses grant letter grades, although all respondents reported that these courses grant academic credit. According to the results of these responses, students in nursing courses receive a higher number of credits than students in most other disciplines, with 35% of respondents indicating that students are granted four credits upon the course's completion. Respondents reported that the credit is treated as a major requirement and nearly 90% of respondents said these nursing courses are offered for one semester.

"A greater number of nursing courses than those in other disciplines except one are reportedly taught by instructional teams."

These nursing courses, as reported, are designed with the greatest variety of instructional techniques of all courses represented in the survey. Major projects and oral presentations are the most frequently reported assignments in nursing courses. These courses also are reported to require final examinations, leadership training, group projects, internships, and portfolio development. Nursing students, according to these results, are required to complete a service-learning project more frequently than students in other disciplines, although the number of respondents who indicated this is still just 20%. The least likely instructional technique to be encountered by students in these courses, are reported to be educational travel, work shadowing, employment, and consideration of graduate school. Respondents noted that all students enrolled in these courses are required to be there, and they said most of these courses have been offered for up to 20 years. Seventy five percent of the respondents indicated that the courses are evaluated, mostly by the students who enroll in them, and 40% of the respondents said these courses are part of comprehensive assessment.

Physical Sciences and Mathematics

Seventeen physical science or mathematics courses were described by survey respondents, half from private institutions and all from institutions of medium selectivity. More than half were from institutions enrolling between 1,001 and 5,000 students. Respondents indicated just three primary goals for these courses, the smallest number of goals in the sample of discipline- and department-based courses. Most of the respondents indicated that these courses are intended to help students integrate and synthesize their learning in the academic major, three of the courses are reported primarily to seek to enhance a particular set of academic skills, and one respondent indicated that the course seeks, above all other goals, to facilitate personal adjustment. Close to 80% of respondents said these courses are taught by faculty members working alone, more than 90% of respondents indicated that each section of these courses enroll fewer than 30 students, all indicated that these courses are letter graded, and most noted that physical science and mathematics courses grant academic credit. Nearly 40% of the respondents indicated that students receive four semester credits for enrolling in the courses, which, respondents said, are treated as major requirements by most institutions. Nearly 80% of respondents said the courses are offered for one semester.

"More than 85% of respondents indicated that these courses require an oral presentation, the most frequently reported instructional technique."

More than 85% of respondents indicated that these courses require an oral presentation, the most frequently reported instructional technique. The next most commonly reported technique is a major project, followed by group project, thesis, and final examination. None of the respondents reported that students in these physical science and mathematics courses engage in work shadowing, employment, or leadership training. According to this survey, these students are also unlikely to encounter service learning, educational travel, and consideration of graduate school. Slightly over 55% of the respondents indicated that these courses require students to enroll in them and 90% of respondents said these courses have been offered on their campuses for up to 20 years. Nearly 80% of respondents indicated that evaluation occurs in these courses, mostly by students, and just over 35% of respondents noted that these courses are involved in comprehensive assessment.

Social Sciences

A total of 51 social science courses were described by survey respondents, half from public institutions and most from medium selectivity institutions. A broad range of institutions were represented. All but 10 of the respondents indicated fostering integration and synthesis within the academic major as the primary goal for social science senior seminars and capstone courses. Six or fewer respondents indicated that these courses are chiefly interested in any other goal. Six respondents each reported that integrating the academic major and work and enhancing students' preparation and prospects for postgraduate education were primarily important in the courses they described. Just over 85% of respondents indicated that these courses are taught by faculty members working alone, close to 90% of respondents said each section of these social sciences courses enroll fewer than 30 students, most of the respondents noted that the courses are letter graded, and all respondents said social science senior seminars and capstone courses grant academic credit. Nearly 75% of respondents said the students receive three semester credits for enrolling in these courses, which are treated as major requirements by most institutions. Nearly 80% of respondents said these courses are offered for one semester.

"...students are least likely to encounter any assignments related to the work place, educational travel, service learning, and alumni involvement or networking."

Close to 85% of respondents indicated that these courses require an oral presentation, the most frequently reported instructional technique. The next most commonly reported technique is a major project, followed much farther behind by final examination, and thesis. According to respondents, students are least likely to encounter any assignments related to the work place, educational travel, service learning, and alumni involvement or networking. Slightly over 80% of respondents said these courses require students to enroll in them and 75% of respondents said these courses have been offered for 15 or fewer years. More than 80% of respondents said evaluations are conducted in these courses, most frequently by students, and just over 35% of respondents said these courses are involved in comprehensive assessment.

Summary of Analysis Across Discipline Clusters

Respondents to this survey described discipline- and department-based senior seminars and capstone courses that are remarkable in their similarity across the disciplines. In all nine discipline clusters, respondents indicated that most of these courses are held for one semester and are offered for three major requirement credits. Most of these courses are reported to be evaluated by their students and 50% or fewer of the respondents, across disciplines, indicated that these courses are included in a comprehensive assessment effort. Responses indicated that, across disciplines, these courses are uniform in their goals. At the top of the list, fostering integration and synthesis within the academic majors was reported as most important in discipline-and department-based courses a total of 308 times. Respondents were nearly four times more likely to mark integration and synthesis within the academic major than they were promoting the coherence and relevance of general education. Twice as many respondents marked integration within the academic major as a goal than they did promoting integration and connections between general education and the academic major.

"Respondents were nearly four times more likely to mark integration and synthesis within the academic major than they were promoting the coherence and relevance of general education."

The next most frequently listed primary goal was promoting integration and connections between the academic major and work world, with 60 total respondents listing this as the single most important goal for these courses. All other goals were each listed as primary on fewer than 30 surveys.

Across all disciplines, respondents who described discipline- or department-based senior seminars and capstone courses were least likely to mark as a goal of the course they were describing promoting effective life planning and decision making. In terms of instructional strategies, few instructors across all disciplines are reported to employ techniques beyond the oral presentation and major project. There are notable exceptions in this and other areas, as discussed below.

Responses indicate that instructors in education and nursing use the greatest variety of techniques for teaching their courses, including team teaching. While integration of the academic major and the world of work is reported to be a primary goal of courses in all disciplines, only education courses ask students to complete assignments that take them to the career center. Notably, however, respondents indicated that none of the top four instructional strategies of any course in any discipline, including education, provides students with the opportunity to go into the work place either to engage in work shadowing, to volunteer, or to work for wages.

"Nursing students in senior seminars and capstone courses, according to the results of this survey, are the most likely to engage in service learning."

Results of this survey indicate that business and management senior seminars and capstone courses are larger than those offered by all other disciplines and more of these courses are reported to be taught by individual faculty members, not by instructional teams. At the high end, 90% of respondents indicated that courses are taught by business and management instructors working alone. At the low end, 50% of respondents who reported on courses in education said instructors in these senior seminars and capstone courses instruct alone. These instructors, respondents suggested, are just as likely to work in teams.

Portfolio development is reportedly a favorite instructional strategy in pre-professional degree program senior seminars and capstone courses, including education and journalism and communications, and is also employed by humanities instructors. This strategy does not lead other respondents' lists.

Nursing students in senior seminars and capstone courses, according to the results of this survey, are the most likely to engage in service learning, although only 20% of respondents said these students are involved in this activity. The next highest percentage of students involved in this activity are reportedly in education and journalism and communications. Overall, this survey indicates that service learning is not commonly employed in discipline- and department-based senior seminars and capstone courses. The least likely students to engage in such an activity as part of these courses, according to these results, are in engineering. And finally, with regard to instructional strategies, only senior seminars and capstone courses in the social sciences and physical sciences and mathematics list thesis among their top four instructional strategies.

In terms of assessment, responses to this survey indicate that senior seminars and capstone courses in the biological sciences are half as likely to be part of a comprehensive assessment effort than humanities courses, the discipline reportedly most likely to be engaged in such an activity. Half of the humanities courses reported on in this survey are part of such an effort.

Chapter 4

Survey Results for Interdisciplinary Courses

One hundred and forty one respondents described senior seminars and capstone courses they identified as interdisciplinary. As noted in Chapter 3, these courses, as depicted by respondents, are, in many respects, more like single discipline- and department-based courses than they are different from them. For example, of the 121 respondents who provided a description of the administering department for interdisciplinary courses, 74 (61%) indicated that they were overseen by individual academic departments. Only 19 (13%) of those 121 respondents noted that more than one academic department collaboratively administered these courses. Thirteen (10%) of the respondents reported that these courses are administered by a central academic affairs office and seven (5.7%) indicated that a general education office administered these courses.

Table 4.1
Percentage of Total of Interdisciplinary Courses by Institution Type (N = 141)

	Institution Type	
	Public	Private
Number	48	93
Percentage	34%	66%

As noted in Table 4.1, a far greater number of respondents who reported on interdisciplinary courses are from private institutions.

The greatest percentage of these respondents are from the smallest institutions (Table 4.2). Only 25.5% of the respondents who described interdisciplinary courses are from institutions enrolling 5,001 or more students. More than 70% of the respondents who described interdisciplinary courses are from institutions of medium selectivity (Table 4.3).

Table 4.2
Percentage of Total of Interdisciplinary Courses by Institution Enrollment Level (N = 141)

	Enrollment Level			
	1,000 and Under	1,001-5,000	5,001-10,000	Over 10,000
Number	49	56	14	22
Percentage	34.8	39.7%	9.9%	15.6%

Table 4.3
Percentage of Total of Interdisciplinary Courses by Institution Selectivity (N = 141)

	Selectivity		
	High	Medium	Low
Number	12	101	28
Percentage	8.5%	71.6%	19.9%

"The greatest percentage of these respondents are from the smallest institutions."

Table 4.4

Number One Goal of Interdisciplinary Courses by Institution Type (N = 141)

Goal	Institution Type	
	Public	Private
Fostering integration and synthesis within the academic major	20.8%	15%
Promoting integration and connections between the academic major and work world	12.4%	4.3%
Improving seniors' career preparation and pre-professional development	4.1%	3.2%
Promoting integration and connections between general education and the academic major	2%**	20.4%
Promoting the coherence and relevance of general education	29.1%	23.6%
Explicitly and intentionally developing important student skills, competencies, and perspectives which are tacitly or incidentally developed in the college curriculum (e.g., leadership skills)	2%	5.3%
Other	4.1%	11.8%
Promoting effective life planning and decision making with respect to issues that will be encountered in adult life after college	2%	6.4%
Enhancing seniors' preparation and prospects for postgraduate education	2%	1%
Enhancing awareness of and support for key personal adjustments encountered by seniors during their transition from college to post-college life	0	1%

Note. Totals do not add to 100%. Some respondents selected more than one number one goal.

**$p<.01$

1. Course Goals

Respondents who described interdisciplinary courses were more likely to list a focus on promoting the coherence and relevance of general education in these senior seminars or capstone courses than respondents who described discipline or department-based courses or all course types combined. Respondents from private institutions were much more likely than respondents from public institutions to report as a number one goal for these courses promoting integration and connections between general education and the academic major (Table 4.4). Only 2% of respondents from public institutions indicated this goal as primarily important. Promoting integration and connections between the academic major and world of work is, according to these responses, a more important goal of public institution interdisciplinary courses than it is for those at private institutions.

Across institution enrollment levels, a negative correlation appeared between size of institutions and selection of integrating general education and the academic major as a number one goal (Table 4.5). Respondents from the smallest institutions were the most likely to mark this as a goal. These survey respondents across enrollment levels were least likely to mark promoting effective life planning and decision making, enhancing seniors' preparation for postgraduate education, and enhancing awareness and support for key personal adjustment issues. In terms of selectivity, respondents from highly selective institutions were least likely to mark promoting integration and connections between the academic major and the work world, and most likely to mark promoting the coherence and relevance of general education.

Table 4.5

Number One Goal of Interdisciplinary Courses by Institution Enrollment Level (N= 141)

Goal	Enrollment Level			
	1,000 and Under	1,001-5,000	5,001-10,000	Over 10,000
Fostering integration and synthesis within the academic major	16.3%	21.4%	14.2%	9%
Promoting integration and connections between the academic major and work world	6.1%	10.7%	7.1%	0
Improving seniors' career preparation and pre-professional development	0	7.1%	0	4.5%
Promoting integration and connections between general education and the academic major	24.4%	10.7%	7.1%	4.5%
Promoting the coherence and relevance of general education	26.5%**	14.2%	57.1%	31.8%
Explicitly and intentionally developing important student skills, competencies, and perspectives which are tacitly or incidentally developed in the college curriculum (e.g., leadership skills)	4%	1.7%	14.2%	4.5%
Other	8.1%	12.5%	7.1%	4.5%
Promoting effective life planning and decision making with respect to issues that will be encountered in adult life after college	6.1%	7.1%	0	0
Enhancing seniors' preparation and prospects for postgraduate education	2%	1.7%	0	0
Enhancing awareness of and support for key personal adjustments encountered by seniors during their transition from college to post-college life	2%	0	0	0

Note. Totals do not add to 100%. Some respondents selected more than one number one goal.

**$p<.01$

Table 4.6

Number One Goal of Interdisciplinary Courses by Institution Selectivity (N = 141)

Goal	Selectivity		
	High	Medium	Low
Fostering integration and synthesis within the academic major	8.3%	18.8%	14.2%
Promoting integration and connections between the academic major and work world	0**	3.9%	21.4%
Improving seniors' career preparation and pre-professional development	0	3.9%	3.5%
Promoting integration and connections between general education and the academic major	8.3%	13.8%	17.8%
Promoting the coherence and relevance of general education	33.3%	26.7%	17.8%
Explicitly and intentionally developing important student skills, competencies, and perspectives which are tacitly or incidentally developed in the college curriculum (e.g., leadership skills)	0	2.9%	10.7%
Other	16.6%	9.9%	3.5%
Promoting effective life planning and decision making with respect to issues that will be encountered in adult life after college	0	5.9%	3.5%
Enhancing seniors' preparation and prospects for postgraduate education	0	.99%	3.5%
Enhancing awareness of and support for key personal adjustments encountered by seniors during their transition from college to post-college life	0	.99%	0

Note. Totals do not add to 100%. Some respondents selected more than one number one goal.

**$p<.01$

Respondents from institutions of medium and low selectivity were more likely than respondents from highly selective institutions to mark general education as a number one goal as it related to the academic major (Table 4.6). Across all three key variables, fostering integration and synthesis within the academic major appeared as a number one goal of interdisciplinary courses for between 9% and 21.4% of respondents.

2. Instructional Responsibility

Respondents from public institutions who reported on interdisciplinary senior seminars and capstone courses indicated that faculty members are almost three times as likely to teach these courses alone than they are to teach them in instructional teams (Table 4.7). Faculty members at private institutions, respondents reported, are nearly as likely to teach interdisciplinary courses in teams as they are to teach them alone. Consistent with the practices reported for discipline- and department-based courses, instructors of interdisciplinary courses were not likely to be non-faculty members. Graduate students are reportedly just as likely to teach these courses as non-career center student affairs professionals.

Respondents reported that faculty members at the smallest institutions and those at institutions with total student enrollments of between 5,001 and 10,000 are nearly as likely to teach in teams as they are to teach alone.

Table 4.7

Instructional Responsibility for Interdisciplinary Courses by Institution Type (N = 141)

Instructional staff	Exclusive Responsibility		As Part of a Team	
	Public	Private	Public	Private
Faculty	62.5%	49.4%	22.9%	39.7%
Career professionals	4.1%	2.1%	0	0
Community leaders	2%	1%	4.1%	1%
Other	0	1%	0	2.1%
Other student affairs professionals	2%	0	0	0
Graduate students	2%	0	0	0

Note. Totals do not add to 100%. Some sections of the same courses are taught by different individuals. Comparisons are between exclusive responsibility versus team approach within institution types.

Table 4.8

Instructional Responsibility for Interdisciplinary Courses by Institution Enrollment Level (N = 141)

Instructional Staff	Exclusive Responsibility				As Part of a Team			
	1,000 and Under	1,001-5,000	5,001-10,000	Over 10,000	1,000 and Under	1,001-5,000	5,001-10,000	Over 10,000
Faculty	42.8%	66.6%	50%	50%	51%	25%	35.7%	18%
Career professionals	0	1.7%	7.1%	9%	0	0	0	0
Community leaders	0	1.7%	0	4.5%	0	3.5%	0	4.5%
Other	0	0	4.5%	0	0	0	0	0
Other student affairs professionals	0	0	0	4.5%	0	0	0	0
Graduate students	0	0	0	4.5%	0	0	0	0

Note. Totals do not add to 100%. Some sections of the same courses are taught by different individuals. Comparisons are between exclusive responsibility versus team approach within institutions with the same enrollment levels.

Respondents from institutions with total student enrollments of between 1,001 and 5,000 and over 10,000 indicated that faculty members are much more likely to teach these courses alone (Table 4.8).

In terms of institutional selectivity, respondents at institutions of low selectivity reported that faculty instructors are more likely to work in teams than to instruct alone. Faculty members at institutions of high and medium selectivity are more likely to instruct these courses alone (Table 4.9).

Table 4.9

Instructional Responsibility for Interdisciplinary Courses by Institution Selectivity (N = 141)

	Exclusive Responsibility			As Part of a Team		
Instructional Staff	High	Medium	Low	High	Medium	Low
Faculty	58.3%	56.4%**	42.8%	33.3%	29.7%	50%
Career professionals	0	2.9%	3.5%	0	0	0
Community leaders	0	.99%	3.5%	0	1.9%	3.5%
Other	0	.99%	0	8.3%	.99	0
Other student affairs professionals	0	0	3.5%	0	0	0
Graduate students	0	0	3.5%	0	0	0

Note. Totals do not add to 100%. Some sections of the same courses are taught by different individuals. Comparisons are between exclusive responsibility versus team approach within institutions of the same selectivity levels.

**$p<.01$

"...respondents at institutions of low selectivity reported that faculty instructors are more likely to work in teams than to instruct alone."

Table 4.10

Maximum Section Enrollments of Interdisciplinary Courses by Institution Type (N = 141)

Enrollment Range	Institution Type	
	Public	Private
0-9	14.5%	19.3%
10-19	12.5%	32.2%
20-29	35.4%	32.2%
30-39	14.5%	9.6%
40-49	8.3%	3.2%
50-75	12.5%	2.1%
76-99	2%	1%
100+	0	0

$p<.01$

3. Course Enrollment Levels

Sections of interdisciplinary senior seminars and capstone courses at public institutions are reported in this survey to be larger than sections of courses at private institutions (Table 4.10).

Maximum section enroll-
ments across institutions of
various sizes are reportedly
similar (Table 4.11), although
the percentage of respon-
dents from larger institutions
who indicated section enrollments of 50 to 75 students
was somewhat greater. Ten
percent of respondents from
medium selectivity institutions indicated that maximum
enrollments in sections of
their interdisciplinary courses
are between 50 and 100
students.

Table 4.11

Maximum Section Enrollments in Interdisciplinary Courses by Institution Enrollment Level (N = 141)

Enrollment Range	Enrollment Level			
	1,000 and Under	1,001-5,000	5,001-10,000	Over 10,000
0-9	12.2%	17.8%	21.4%	27.2%
10-19	36.7%	25%	14.2%	9%
20-29	40.8%	32.1%	28.5%	22.7%
30-39	4%	16%	21.4%	9%
40-49	6.1%	1.7%	0	13.6%
50-75	0	5.3%	14.2%	13.6%
76-99	0	1.7%	0	4.5%
100+	0	0	0	0

Table 4.12

Maximum Section Enrollments in Interdisciplinary Courses by Institution Selectivity (N = 141)

Enrollment Range	Selectivity		
	High	Medium	Low
0-9	25%	17.8%	14.2%
10-19	25%	24.7%	28.5%
20-29	33.3%	31.6%	39.2%
30-39	16.6%	11.8%	7.1%
40-49	0	4.9%	7.1%
50-75	0	6.9%	3.5%
76-99	0	1.9%	0
100+	0	0	0

Those percentages are lower at institutions of low selectivity and the largest section size at highly selective institutions is reported to be between 30 and 39 students (Table 4.12).

4. Amount and Type of Academic Credit and Grading Practices

According to this survey, interdisciplinary senior seminars and capstone courses carry more academic credit at public institutions than those at private institutions (Table 4.13). The majority of these courses are still reported by respondents to carry three semester credits. Public institutions are reported more often to grant one and two semester credit hours for these courses than private institutions.

Table 4.13

Amount of Credit Granted by Interdisciplinary Courses by Institution Type (N = 121)

Credit Hours	Institution Type	
	Public	Private
One qtr.	0	0
Two qtrs.	0	2.4%
Three qtrs.	0	0
Four qtrs.	2.5%	1.2%
Five qtrs.	5.1%	0
Six or more qtrs.	0	0
One sem.	2.5%	10.9%
Two sems.	2.5%	13.4%
Three sems.	53.8%	59.7%
Four or more sems.	33.3%	12.2%

$p < .01$

Table 4.14

Amount of Credit Granted by Interdisciplinary Courses by Institution Enrollment Level (N = 121)

Credits Hours	Enrollment Level			
	1,000 and Under	1,001-5,000	5,001-10,000	Over 10,000
One qtr.	0	0	0	0
Two qtrs.	0	0	0	1.6%
Three qtrs.	0	0	0	0
Four qtrs.	2.2	0	9%	0
Five qtrs.	0	1.9%	0	7.1
Six or more qtrs.	0	0	0	0
One sem.	8.8%	9.8%	0	7.1%
Two sems.	17.7%	7.8%	0	0
Three sems.	53.3%	60.7%	45.4%	71.4%
Four or more sems.	17.7%	19.6%	45.4%	0

p<.01

In terms of institution size, respondents reported similar practices in terms of the amount of academic credit carried by these courses, with one exception. No respondents reported that courses at institutions with total student enrollments over 10,000 award four or more semester credits for these courses (Table 4.14). Courses at highly selective institutions represented in this survey are reported to carry four or more semester credits far more frequently than courses at low and medium selectivity institutions. Responses indicate that courses at medium and low selectivity institutions more often carry one to three semester credits.

"Courses at highly selective institutions represented in this survey are reported to carry four or more semester credits far more frequently than courses at low and medium selectivity institutions."

The majority of survey respondents who reported on interdisciplinary senior seminars and capstone courses report that these courses, across institution types, grant credit, and that they are letter graded. Twenty percent of respondents from private institutions and 27% of respondents from public institutions reported that these courses are treated as general education requirements, a departure from the reported practices in discipline- and department-based courses and the other three course types reported on in Chapter 5.

Table 4.15

Amount of Credit Granted by Interdisciplinary Courses by Institution Selectivity (N = 121)

	Selectivity		
Credit Hours	High	Medium	Low
One qtr.	0	0	0
Two qtrs.	0	2.2%	0
Three qtrs.	0	0	0
Four qtrs.	0	1.1%	4.5%
Five qtrs.	0	1.1%	4.5%
Six or more qtrs.	0	0	0
One sem.	0	7.8%	13.6%
Two sems.	0	7.8%	22.7%
Three sems.	20%	66.2%	40.9%
Four or more sems.	80%	13.4%	13.6%

$p < .01$

Table 4.16
Type of Credit Granted by Interdisciplinary Courses by Institution Type (N = 141)

	Institution Type	
Granting Credit	Public	Private
Yes	87.%	91.4%
No	12.5%	8.6%

	Institution Type	
Type of Grade	Public	Private
Pass/fail	4.1%	5.3%
Letter grade	95.8%	94.6%

	Institution Type	
Credit Applied As	Public	Private
Core requirement	45.8%	59.1%
Elective	4.1%	3.2%
Major requirement	14.5%	13.9%
General education requirement	27%	20.4%
Other	8.3%	3.2%

As reported, these interdisciplinary courses are most likely to be part of core requirements, and fewer than 15% of respondents from both public and private institutions indicated that these courses are treated as major requirements (Table 4.18). Less than 75% of respondents from institutions with total enrollments of more than 10,000 students indicated that interdisciplinary senior seminars and capstone courses carry academic credit compared to more than 90% of respondents at institutions enrolling 1,000 and fewer students and those enrolling up to 10,000 students.

Nearly all respondents to this survey indicated that these courses are letter graded. The smallest institutions are reported by 71.4% of those respondents to consider these courses part of core require- ments, a designation far more likely than at other sized institutions. Courses at other institutions are reportedly more likely to consider these courses major requirements. Between 19.6% and 35.7% of respondents from various institution sizes indicated that these courses fulfill general education requirements (Table 4.17). Across selectivity levels, respondents reported that most interdisciplinary senior seminars and capstone courses carry academic credit and most are letter graded.

Table 4.17

Type of Credit Granted by Interdisciplinary Courses by Institution Enrollment Level (N = 141)

	Enrollment Level			
Granting Credit	1,000 and Under	1,001-5,000	5,001-10,000	Over 10,000
Yes	91.8%	94.6%	92.8%	72.7%
No	8.1%	5.3%	7.1%	27.2

$p<.05$

	Enrollment Level			
Type of Grade	1,000 and Under	1,001-5,000	5,001-10,000	Over 10,000
Pass/Fail	2%	7.1%	7.1%	4.5%
Letter grade	97.9%	92.8%	92.8%	95.4%

	Enrollment Level			
Credit Applied As	1,000 and Under	1,001-5,000	5,001-10,000	Over 10,000
Core requirement	71.4%	44.6%	35.7%	54.5%
Elective	0	7.1%	7.1%	0
Major requirement	6.1%	23.2%	14.2%	9%
General education requirement	20.4%	19.6%	35.7%	27.2%
Other	2%	5.3%	7.1%	9%

Table 4.18
*Type of Credit Granted by Interdisciplinary Courses by
Institution Selectivity (N = 141)*

	Selectivity		
Granting Credit	High	Medium	Low
Yes	91.6%	90.1%	89.2%
No	8.3%	9.9%	10.7%

	Selectivity		
Type of Grade	High	Medium	Low
Pass/fail	0	5.9%	3.5%
Letter grade	100%	94%	96%

	Selectivity		
Credit Applied As	High	Medium	Low
Core requirement	25%	55.4%	64.2%
Elective	8.3%	3.9%	0
Major requirement	25%	10.8%	21.4%
General education requirement	33.3%	24.7%	10.7%
Other	8.3%	4.9%	3.5%

How the credit for these courses applies is reported to be different across institutions of different selectivity levels. Institutions of medium selectivity are reported by the respondents to be more likely than institutions of other selectivity levels to treat these courses as core requirements and general education requirements; low selectivity institutions are reportedly more likely than other institutions to treat these courses as core requirements and major requirements. Responses from highly selective institutions indicate that these institutions are almost evenly divided in the approach they take to applying credit. Respondents report that these courses are treated as core requirements, major requirements, and general education requirements (Table 4.18).

5. Length of Course

Most interdisciplinary senior seminars and capstone courses, across institution types, institution enrollment levels, and institution selectivity levels are reported by these survey respondents to be one academic term in length—either one quarter or one semester (Tables 4.19, 4.20, and 4.21). More respondents from institutions over 10,000 and from medium and low selectivity institutions indicated that these courses are one quarter in length.

Table 4.19
Length of Interdisciplinary Courses by Institution Type (N = 126)

Length of Courses	Institution Type	
	Public	Private
1-8 weeks	2.3%	3.5%
1 quarter	7.1%	4.7%
1 semester	85.7%	86.9%
2 quarters	0	0
2 semesters	4.7%	4.7%

Table 4.20
Length of Interdisciplinary Courses by Institution Enrollment Level (N = 126)

Length of Course	Enrollment Level			
	1,000 and Under	1,001-5,000	5,001-10,000	Over 10,000
1-8 weeks	2.1%	3.9%	0	6.2%
1 quarter	4.3%	1.9%	7.6%	18.7%
1 semester	89.1%	88.2%	92.3%	68.7%
2 quarters	0	0	0	0
2 semesters	4.3%	5.8%	0	6.2%

Table 4.21

Length of Interdisciplinary Courses by Institution Selectivity (N = 126)

Length of Course	Selectivity		
	High	Medium	Low
1-8 weeks	0	4.4%	0
1 quarter	0	4.4%	11.5%
1 semester	100%	86.6%	80.7%
2 quarters	0	0	0
2 semesters	0	4.4%	7.6%

6. Administrative Responsibility

As noted at the beginning of this chapter, interdisciplinary senior seminars and capstone courses represented in this survey are reported to be administered by individual academic departments and, in some instances, they are reported to be collaboratively administered by more than one academic department. A higher percentage of respondents indicated such a collaborative arrangement for interdisciplinary courses than respondents who described any other course type.

7. Instructional Practices

Respondents who described interdisciplinary senior seminars and capstone courses reported instructional practices in these courses similar to those favored in courses of other types. Oral presentations and major projects are the most frequently reported instructional approach in these courses.

Courses at public institutions are reportedly more likely to require final examinations, group projects, and internships than courses at private institutions (Table 4.22). Interdisciplinary senior seminars and capstone courses at private institutions are reportedly more likely to require thesis writing. Differences are reportedly not great among the most favored instructional practices across institutions of varying sizes.

Table 4.22

Instructional Components of Interdisciplinary Courses by Institution Type (N = 141)

Instructional Component	Frequency of Use by Institution Type	
	Public	Private
Oral presentation	66.6%	70.9%
Major project	66.6%	51.6%
Group project	47.9%	40.8%
Final exam	50%	33.3%
Portfolio development	18.7%	22.5%
Thesis	16.6%	23.6%
Use of career center	6.2%	5.3%
Internship	10.4%	4.3%
Other	20.8%	12.9%
Explicit consideration of graduate school	2%	4.3%
Alumni involvement/networking	8.3%	10.7%
Leadership training	8.3%	8.6%
Service learning/community service	16.6%	11.8%
Educational travel	6.2%	1%
Employment (remunerative/non-remunerative)	4.1%	2.1%
Work shadowing	6.2%	1%

Note. Totals do not add to 100%. Respondents were asked to choose all that applied.

Table 4.23

Instructional Components of Interdisciplinary Courses by Institution Enrollment Level (N = 141)

Instructional Component	Frequency of Use by Enrollment Level			
	1,000 and Under	1,001-5,000	5,001-10,000	Over 10,000
Oral presentation	67.3%	78.5%	71.4%	50%
Major project	53%	62.5%	57.1%	50%
Group project	36.7%	48.2%	42.8%	45.4%
Final exam	30.6%	37.5%	57.1%	50%
Portfolio development	30.6%	19.6%	21.4%	4.5%
Thesis	30.6%	17.8%	28.5%	4.5%
Use of career center	0	8.9%	14.2%	4.5%
Internship	2%	7.1%	14.2%	9%
Other	10.2%	16%	35.7%	13.6%
Explicit consideration of graduate school	4%	5.3%	0	0
Alumni involvement/ networking	2%**	21.4%	7.1%	0
Leadership training	10.2%	7.1%	7.1%	9%
Service learning/ community service	4%	19.6%	7%	22.7%
Educational travel	2%	1.7%	14.2%	0
Employment (remunerative/ non-remunerative)	0	7.1%	0	0
Work shadowing	0	3.5%	7.1%	4.5%

Note. Totals do not add to 100%. Respondents were asked to choose all that applied.

**p<.01

The widest gap respondents reported involves portfolio development and required thesis writing. Portfolio development is used by 30.6% of respondents from the smallest institutions, while only 4.5% of respondents from the largest institutions indicated the same. Required thesis writing is reported by 30.6% of respondents to be used in courses at the smallest institutions, contrasted to only 4.5% of respondents who indicated the same for courses at the largest institutions.

A wide gap was also reported for service learning. Four percent of respondents from the smallest institutions indicated that this approach is used, while 22.7% of respondents from the largest institutions reported use of this approach (Table 2.23).

The widest variations between responses across institution selectivity level regarded portfolio development (no respondents from highly selective institutions indicated that this approach is employed), internships (respondents from institutions of low selectivity were more likely to indicate this approach), leadership training, and service learning (no respondents from highly selective institutions reported that these approaches are used in interdisciplinary senior seminars and capstone courses).

Table 4.24

Instructional Components of Interdisciplinary Courses by Institution Selectivity (N = 141)

	Frequency of Use by Selectivity		
Instructional Component	High	Medium	Low
Oral presentation	58.3%	71.2%	67.8%
Major project	41.6%	56.4%	64.2%
Group project	50%	42.5%	42.8%
Final exam	25%	40.5%	39.2%
Portfolio development	0	22.7%	25%
Thesis	8.3%	23.7%	17.8%
Use of career center	0	5.9%	7.1%
Internship	8.3%	3.9%	14.2%
Other	41.6%*	14.8%	7.1%
Explicit consideration of graduate school	8.3%	2.9%	3.5%
Alumni involvement/networking	8.3%	10.8%	7.1%
Leadership training	0	6.9%	17.8%
Service learning/community service	0	15.8%	10.7%
Educational travel	0	3.9%	0
Employment (remunerative/non-remunerative)	0	1.9%	7.1%
Work shadowing	0	1.9%	7.1%

Note. Totals do not add to 100%. Respondents were asked to choose all that applied.

*p<.05

Table 4.25
*Students Required to Take Interdisciplinary Courses by
Institution Type (N = 141)*

| | Institution Type | |
Students Required to Take Course	Public	Private
All	75%	78.4%
Some	20.8%	17.2%
None	4.1%	4.3%

Table 4.26
*Students Required to Take Interdisciplinary Courses by
Institution Enrollment Level (N = 141)*

| | Enrollment Level | | | |
Students Required to Take Course	1,000 and Under	1,001-5,000	5,001-10,000	Over 10,000
All	75.5%	76.7%	78.5%	81.8%
Some	24.4%	16%	14.2%	13.6%
None	0	7.1%	7.1%	4.5%

8. Populations Required to Take the Course

Responses to this survey indicate that fewer students are required to take interdisciplinary senior seminars and capstone courses than are required to enroll in discipline- and department-based courses. Practices in this regard are reported to be similar across institution types and institution enrollment levels (Tables 4.25 and 4.26).

The greatest differences in this regard are reported across institutions of differing selectivity levels. While 66.6% of respondents from highly selective institutions indicated that all students are required to enroll in interdisciplinary senior seminars and capstone courses, 77.2% from institutions of medium selectivity indicated the same, and 82.1% of respondents from institutions of low selectivity reported that all students are required to take these courses (Table 4.27).

Table 4.27
Students Required to Take Interdisciplinary Courses by Institution Selectivity (N = 141)

Students Required to Take Course	Selectivity		
	High	Medium	Low
All	66.6%	77.2%	82.1%
Some	16.6%	18.8%	17.8%
None	16.6%	3.9%	0

Table 4.28
Gender Ratio of Interdisciplinary Courses by Institution Type (N = 26)

Gender Ratio	Institution Type	
	Public	Private
70% women	10%	6.2%
50 – 70% women	30%	50%
50/50	30%	25%
50 – 70% men	30%	6.2%
70% men	0	12.5%

Note. Applies only to elective courses.

Table 4.29
Gender Ratio of Interdisciplinary Courses by Institution Enrollment Level (N = 26)

	Enrollment Level			
Gender Ratio	1,000 and Under	1,001-5,000	5,001-10,000	Over 10,000
70% women	0	18.1%	0	0
50 – 70% women	40%	54.5%	66.6%	14.2%
50/50	40%	18.1%	33.3%	28.5%
50 – 70% men	0	9%	0	42.8%
70% men	20%	0	0	14.2%

Note. Applies only to elective courses.

Table 4.30
Gender Ratio of Interdisciplinary Courses by Institution Selectivity (N = 26)

	Selectivity		
Gender Ratio	High	Medium	Low
70% women	0	10%	0
50 – 70% women	66.6%	40%	33.3%
50/50	33.3%	20%	66.6%
50 – 70% men	0	20%	0
70% men	0	10%	0

Note. Applies only to elective courses.

Respondents indicated that when these courses are offered as electives, they are more often subscribed to by women than by men. Men at public institutions are reportedly more likely to enroll voluntarily in these courses than men at private institutions (Table 4.28).

Men are also reported to enroll voluntarily more often at the largest institutions than men at institutions of other sizes (Table 4.29), and men at medium selectivity institutions are reported to be more likely to enroll voluntarily in these courses than men at institutions of other selectivity levels (Table 4.30).

9. Length of Existence at the Institution

As reported by these respondents, interdisciplinary senior seminars and capstone courses at private institutions have existed for up to 50 years, while courses at public institutions are reported to have existed for 30 years or less (Table 4.31).

Table 4.31

Length of Existence at Institution of Interdisciplinary Courses by Institution Type (N= 120)

| | Institution Type | |
Range of Years	Public	Private
< 1	2.5%	2.5%
1-5	17.5%	35%
6-10	22.5%	25%
11-15	12.5%	13.7%
16-20	17.5%	7.5%
21-25	17.5%	5%
26-30	10%	3.7%
31-35	0	2.5%
36-40	0	2.5%
41-45	0	1.2%
46-50	0	1.2%
51-78	0	0

Table 4.32
Length of Existence at Institution of Interdisciplinary Courses by Institution Enrollment Level (N = 120)

Range of Years	Enrollment Level			
	1,000 and Under	1,001-5,000	5,001-10,000	Over 10,000
< 1	2.3%	2%	0	5.8%
1-5	37.2%	28.5%	9%	23.5%
6-10	27.9%	20.4%	9%	35.2%
11-15	13.9%	12.2%	9%	17.6%
16-20	4.6%	10.2%	36.3%	11.7%
21-25	11.6%	8.1%	18.1%	0
26-30	2.3%	8.1%	9%	5.8%
31-35	0	4%	0	0
36-40	0	4%	0	0
41-45	0	0	9%	0
46-50	0	2%	0	0
51-78	0	0	0	0

Responses indicate that there are older interdisciplinary courses at institutions with total enrollments of between 1,001 and 5,000 students than there are at institutions of other sizes (Table 4.32).

Although respondents at medium selectivity institutions reported that a few courses have existed at those institutions for 31 or more years, responses suggest that courses at highly selective institutions are generally the oldest across institutional selectivity levels (Table 4.33).

Table 4.33

Length of Existence at Institution of Interdisciplinary Courses by Institution Selectivity (N = 120)

| Range of Years | Selectivity | | |
	High	Medium	Low
< 1	10%	1.1%	4.3%
1-5	10%	32.1%	26%
6-10	20%	20.6%	39.1%
11-15	0	18.3%	0
16-20	30%	8%	13%
21-25	20%	8%	8%
26-30	10%	4.6%	8%
31-35	0	2.3%	0
36-40	0	2.3%	0
41-45	0	1.1%	0
46-50	0	1.1%	0
51-78	0	0	0

"...responses suggest that courses at highly selective institutions are generally the oldest across institutional selectivity levels."

Table 4.34
Evaluation of Interdisciplinary Courses by Institution
Type (N = 141)

	Institution Type	
Course Evaluated	Public	Private
Yes	77%	79.5%

Table 4.35
Evaluation of Interdisciplinary Courses by Institution
Enrollment Level (N = 141)

	Enrollment Level			
Course Evaluated	1,000 and Under	1,001-5,000	5,001-10,000	Over 10,000
Yes	81.6%	80.3%	78.5%	68.1%

$p < .01$

Table 4.36
Evaluation of Interdisciplinary Courses by Instituton
Selectivity (N = 141)

	Selectivity		
Course Evaluated	High	Medium	Low
Yes	75%	79%	78%

10. Evaluation Practices

Nearly 80% of respondents from public and private institutions indicated that these interdisciplinary courses are evaluated by the students and faculty members who are involved in them (Table 4.34).

A smaller percentage of respondents (68.1%) from institutions with total enrollments of more than 10,000 students indicated that these courses are evaluated. In fact, there is a negative correlation between size of institution and likelihood that interdisciplinary senior seminars and capstone courses will be evaluated (Table 4.35).

Across institutional selectivity levels, at least 75% of the respondents noted that these courses are evaluated (Table 4.36).

"…there is a negative correlation between size of institution and likelihood that interdisciplinary senior seminars and capstone courses will be evaluated ."

11. Assessment Practices

The percentages of respondents who indicated that these courses are involved in comprehensive assessment are higher than for most other course types represented in this survey. A gap appears between the number of respondents who indicated that interdisciplinary senior seminars and capstone courses at public and private institutions are involved in comprehensive assessment, with courses at private institutions reportedly more likely to be involved in such a process than those at public institutions (Table 4.38).

Regarding institutions of various sizes, percentages of respondents who indicated that these courses are involved in assessment range from a low of 28.5% at institutions with total student enrollments of between 5,001 and 10,000 and a high of 71.4% for institutions enrolling a total of 1,000 or fewer students (Table 4.39). A negative correlation exists between institutional selectivity and reported participation of these courses in comprehensive assessment, with courses at the most selective institutions the least likely to be reported to be part of such a process (Table 4.39).

Table 4.37
Assessment Tied to Interdisciplinary Courses by Institution Type (N = 141)

	Institution Type	
Course Tied to Comprehensive Assessment	Public	Private
Yes	47.9%	61.2%

Table 4.38
Assessment Tied to Interdisciplinary Courses by Institution Enrollment Level (N = 141)

	Institution Type			
Course Tied to Comprehensive Assessment	1,000 and Under	1,001-5,000	5,001-10,000	Over 10,000
Yes	71.4%	55.3%	28.5%	45.4%

p<.05

Table 4.39
Assessment Tied to Interdisciplinary Courses by Institution Enrollment Level (N = 141)

	Selectivity		
Course Tied to Comprehensive Assessment	High	Medium	Low
Yes	25%	57%	67%

p<.05

Summary of Analysis – Interdisciplinary Courses

Overall, these results indicate that interdisciplinary courses are similar to other course types represented in this survey with one notable exception. These courses are reported to be somewhat more focused on general education, as a separate topic or as it relates to the academic major, than courses of other types. Respondents from private, highly selective, and small institutions were more likely than other respondents who reported on interdisciplinary courses to indicate that general education, as a topic in its own right, is of primary importance. Respondents who reported on interdisciplinary courses from other institutions were more likely than respondents from highly selective, small, and private institutions to indicate that general education is of importance as it relates to the academic major.

Respondents from public institutions who described interdisciplinary senior seminars and capstone courses were more likely than their private institution counterparts to mark that these courses are intended to prepare students for the world of work. Respondents from highly selective institutions were least likely to mark as primarily important for interdisciplinary courses integrating and connecting the academic major and the world of work.

As with respondents who reported on other course types, respondents who described interdisciplinary courses indicated that faculty members are almost exclusively responsible for instruction of these courses. In a departure from the reported practices in discipline- and department-based courses, faculty members at private institutions are reported to be nearly as likely to teach interdisciplinary senior seminars and capstone courses in teams as they are to teach them alone. This is also indicated to be true for courses at institutions with total student enrollments of 1,000 or under and enrollments between 5,001 and 10,000 students.

"…faculty members at private institutions are reported to be nearly as likely to teach interdisciplinary senior seminars and capstone courses in teams as they are to teach them alone."

Instructors at the lowest selectivity schools are reportedly more likely to teach in teams than they are to teach alone. Graduate students and student affairs professionals outside career centers are reported to be unlikely to instruct these interdisciplinary courses, a consistency seen across most course types.

The largest interdisciplinary course sections reported on in this survey are those at public, medium selectivity, and large institutions. According to this survey, sections of interdisciplinary courses are similar in size to sections of other types of senior seminars and capstone courses. Consistency of practice across course types is also seen in the number of academic credits these courses carry; they are generally offered for three semester credits. Responses indicate that interdisciplinary courses at public institutions tend to carry more credit than those at private institutions. Courses at highly selective institutions are reportedly more likely to carry a higher number of credits than courses at institutions of low and medium selectivity.

"In terms of instructional practices in interdisciplinary senior seminars and capstone courses, this survey indicates that thesis writing distinguishes practices across institutions."

Most of these courses, according to respondents, are granted academic credit and are letter graded. They are generally reported to fulfill core requirements, major requirements, and to a greater extent than discipline- and department-based courses, are reported to fulfill general education requirements, although this last is not the case for a majority of these courses. In most cases, interdisciplinary courses were reported to be one academic term in length.

In terms of instructional practices in interdisciplinary senior seminars and capstone courses, this survey indicates that thesis writing distinguishes practices across institutions. Respondents from private and small institutions were more likely to mark this as an instructional practice of choice than respondents from public and larger institutions. Courses at public institutions are reportedly more likely to include final examinations, group projects, and internships; courses at large institutions are more likely than small institutions to require service learning. Service learning was not a component reported to be part of interdisciplinary senior seminars and capstone courses at highly selective institutions.

Interdisciplinary courses are, according to this survey, not required as often as their discipline- and department-based counterparts, with the least likely interdisciplinary courses to be required reported to be at highly selective institutions. Women are reported to subscribe to elective interdisciplinary courses more often than men. And, according to these responses, men are more likely to volunteer to take these courses at public and large institutions and institutions of medium selectivity than men at other institutions.

Responses to this survey indicate that interdisciplinary senior seminars and capstone courses have existed longer at private institutions than at public institutions, existed longer at institutions with total student enrollments of between 1,001 and 5,000 students than at institutions of other sizes, and existed longer at highly selective institutions than at institutions of other selectivity levels.

These courses are, according to respondents, evaluated most of the time and they are evaluated by students and faculty members involved in the courses. Interdisciplinary courses at the largest institutions are not reported to be evaluated as often as interdisciplinary courses at other size institutions. Assessment practices reported by respondents set interdisciplinary courses apart from most other courses described in this survey. Interdisciplinary courses are reported to be involved in comprehensive institutional assessment more often than courses of other types.

Interdisciplinary courses at private institutions are reportedly more likely to be involved in assessment than interdisciplinary courses at public institutions. More than 70% of respondents from the smallest sized institutions indicated that these courses are involved in comprehensive assessment, and interdisciplinary courses at institutions of the lowest selectivity are reportedly more likely than courses at institutions of other selectivity levels to be involved in this type of assessment process.

"Interdisciplinary courses are reported to be involved in comprehensive institutional assessment more often than courses of other types."

Chapter 5

Survey Results for Transition, Career Planning, and "Other" Courses

In this chapter, findings are summarized for the final three types of courses described by survey respondents, including transition courses, career planning courses, and courses designated as "other" by the respondents. As noted in Chapter 2, only 116 total respondents completed surveys on these three course types combined, prompting a decision to offer this summary in narrative rather than tabular form.

As reported by the respondents, these course types share many characteristics in common with discipline- and department-based courses, with some minor variations. The career planning courses in this survey, as one might expect, are more focused than discipline- and department-based courses on integrating the academic major and the world of work, and they engage students in additional career-related activities. Transition courses reported on in this survey are a more eclectic mix of academic major and post-graduation work-related courses than career planning courses. Respondents indicated that transition courses are administered most often by academic departments and they are reported to offer opportunities for career exploration activities. Across these two course types, the responses indicate that these courses carry fewer academic credits than discipline- and department-based courses and interdisciplinary courses and have a greater mix of instructional staff than discipline- and department-based and interdisciplinary courses. The characteristics of "other" courses reported on by 40 respondents are, in general, closely related to those of the discipline- and department-based courses described in the survey.

Transition Courses

Transition courses were described on the survey instrument for respondents as courses "focusing on preparation for work, graduate school, life choice, life skills, or life after college." Completed surveys describing 50 such courses were returned, 13 of these courses are offered at public institutions and 37 are held at private institutions. Fifteen of the courses are offered at institutions enrolling 1,000 or fewer students. Twenty five courses are offered at institutions of enrollments between 1,001 and 5,000 students, three are held at institutions of between 5,001 and 10,000 students, and seven are offered at institutions with total enrollments of more than 10,000 students. Four of the surveys were returned from highly selective institutions, 40 are from medium selectivity institutions, and six were received from institutions of low selectivity.

The emphasis of these transition courses is reported to be on improving seniors' career preparation and pre-professional development. The second most frequently marked number one goal of these

"According to respondents, faculty and career center professionals are equally likely to instruct transition courses."

courses is promoting integration and connections between the academic major and work world. Other goals related to personal adjustment and life planning follow closely behind. Transition courses reported on in this survey are least concerned with general education.

According to respondents, faculty and career center professionals are equally likely to instruct transition courses, with all other choices of instructors (other student affairs professionals, community and workplace professionals, graduate students, and others), less likely to serve in these roles. In a departure from the practice of other course types, transition courses are just as likely to be taught in teams as they are by individual instructors, with highly selective institutions the most likely to use the team approach. Of the 50 respondents who reported on transition courses, 31 indicated that individual academic departments administer these courses, with the rest split between student affairs divisions and career services units.

Enrollments in transition courses are most often between 20 and 29 students. Public institutions are reportedly less likely than private institutions to assign a letter grade to these courses (75.6% of respondents from private institutions indicated that transition courses are letter graded, as opposed to 61.5% of respondents from public institutions who indicated the same). Although a higher percentage of these private institution courses are reported to assign letter grades than those at public institutions, private institution courses tend to grant credit less often for these courses than their public counterparts.

An inverse correlation exists between selectivity and the practice of granting credit for the transition courses described in this survey, with institutions of lower selectivity assigning more credit. Transition courses in this survey are similar to career planning courses in the number of credits students earn for their enrollment, which is most often one semester credit. Most of the 50 transition courses described in this survey are offered as major requirements or core requirements, with only one of these courses offered as part of the general education curriculum.

When these courses are offered as electives, respondents reported that, like career planning courses, they are more heavily subscribed to by women than men students. However, most of these courses are required for the students who enroll in them, with smaller institutions more likely to require them than institutions enrolling a total of more than 5,000 students. Most of the courses reported on in this survey are offered at schools that organize their terms by semesters; these courses are reported by the respondents to be held for one semester, although 10 of the 40 reported on from respondents at medium selectivity institutions are offered for eight weeks or under.

According to this survey, transition courses are taught using a greater variety of techniques than most of the other courses described. Oral presentation, dominant among discipline- department-based, and interdisciplinary courses, is also reported to be the most widely used instructional technique employed in transition courses. However, in transition courses these techniques are followed closely by use of the career center and development of a portfolio (also reportedly predominant in pre-professional discipline- and department-based courses). Major projects appear high on the respondents' list of instructional components used, just as they do with discipline- and department-based courses, but are accompanied with alumni involvement, networking, and explicit consideration of graduate school (all approaches used in career planning courses).

> *"Major projects appear high on the respondents' list of instructional components used, just as they do with discipline- and department-based courses, but are accompanied with alumni involvement, networking, and explicit consideration of graduate school (all approaches used in career planning courses)."*

Courses at private institutions represented in the survey are more likely than those at public institutions to include a discussion of graduate school and three private institution courses require a thesis, while no public institution courses make this a requirement. Respondents from the largest institutions were just as likely to mark portfolio development and oral presentation as they were to mark use of the career center. According to reports of these respondents, little difference exists between the instructional techniques employed by institutions of various selectivity levels. As with other course types, the least likely components to appear in this survey as part of transition courses are educational travel, service learning, and any activity taking students into the work place.

In the aggregate, these courses have not, according to survey responses, been offered for as many years at their institutions as career planning courses, with a larger percentage offered for one to five years while career planning courses have existed more often for six to 10 years. A total of 76.9% of respondents indicated that courses at public institutions are subjected to an evaluation process, while that percentage was 83.7% for respondents from private institutions. This is lower than the percentages for responses from discipline- and department-based and interdisciplinary courses, and consistent with the percentages for career planning course respondents. Involvement in comprehensive assessment, however, is reported to be higher than it is for most other courses described in this survey. Close to 55% of respondents who reported on courses at public institutions and 30% of respondents who reported on courses from private institutions indicated that transition courses are assessed centrally. There is an inverse correlation between selectivity of an institution and likelihood of these courses being involved in comprehensive assessments, with courses from highly selective institutions reportedly the least likely to be assessed. Responses indicate that, in terms of size of institution, the most likely courses to be involved in central assessment are at the largest institutions, while, near the other end, none of the 15 courses described in surveys returned from institutions enrolling between 5,001 and 10,000 students participate in comprehensive assessment efforts. Overall, 36% of respondents reporting on transition courses said these courses are involved in such an assessment.

Career Planning Courses

The nationwide distribution of surveys to college and university administrators, including all directors of career centers at regionally accredited institutions, yielded only 26 completed surveys describing career planning senior seminars or capstone courses. Survey results reported throughout this monograph suggest that career issues are addressed within other courses. As noted in Chapters 3 and 4, respondents indicated that department- and discipline-based courses and interdisciplinary courses heavily emphasize integrating and connecting the academic major to the world of work, and improving the students' career preparation and pre-professional development.

Of the 26 courses identified in this survey as career planning courses, 10 are offered at public institutions and 16 are held at private institutions. Eight of the courses are offered at institutions with enrollments of 1,000 students or fewer, 11 are from institutions of 1,001 to 5,000, four are from institutions with enrollments of 5,001 to 10,000, and three are from institutions enrolling more than 10,000 students. Two of the career planning courses described are from highly selective institutions, 20 are offered at medium selectivity institutions, and four are offered at institutions of low selectivity.

As might be expected, these courses are reported to be primarily focused on improving seniors' career preparation and pre-professional development. None of the other goals offered as choices to the respondents were reported by them to be as overwhelmingly important in these courses. As has been seen with other types of courses reported on in this survey, general education, as it related to the academic major or as a stand-alone subject, is not a primary goal of the career planning courses described.

These courses are reported to be twice as likely to be taught by individual instructors as they are to be taught by teams of individuals. According to respondents, faculty members are just slightly less likely to offer these courses than the institutions' career center professionals and no student affairs professionals outside of career centers are reported to be involved in these courses. One community/workplace professional appeared among the instructors, as did one graduate student. Less than half of the respondents indicated that these courses are administered through career services units, with the rest reporting that the courses are administered by other student affairs or academic affairs units, or individual academic departments.

"According to respondents, faculty members are just slightly less likely to offer these courses than the institutions' career center professionals and no student affairs professionals outside of career centers are reported to be involved in these courses."

Similar to other course types reported on in this survey, sections of career planning courses are held to enrollments of fewer than 30 students. Results of this survey indicate that courses at public institutions are less likely than those at private institutions to assign a letter grade (87.5% of respondents at private institutions indicated that courses are letter graded, as compared to 70% of respondents at public institutions) and there is a positive correlation between selectivity level of the institution and likelihood of assigning a letter grade to the course. Highly selective and smaller institutions tend, according to this survey, to assign letter grades to these courses. Respondents reported that nearly all of the students who take these courses receive academic credit for them, with students at low selectivity schools being the least likely to receive credit. According to respondents, the career planning courses represented in this survey do not grant as many credits as either the interdisciplinary courses or the discipline- or department-based courses. Most of these courses are reported to grant either one or two credits and respondents indicated that these courses are most often treated as electives, with major requirement being the next most likely designation.

The career planning courses in this survey, when they are offered as electives, are reported to be more heavily subscribed to by women than men students. Consistent with their principal status as electives, most of these courses are reported not to be required for any student population. Most of the career planning courses in this survey are one academic term, either one quarter or one semester, in length. Not surprisingly, the instructional component most often reported to be part of these courses is use of the career center. The next most frequently listed instructional technique is development of a portfolio, followed closely by production of a major project, and delivery of an oral presentation. Alumni involvement, networking and consideration of graduate school are also high on the list of instructional techniques used in these career planning courses. No respondents said that educational travel or development of a thesis are part of these courses, with service learning again not widely reported to be employed.

Notably, the survey indicated that any activity involving students entering the work place, for internships, work shadowing, paid or volunteer employment, is as rare in these career planning courses as educational travel or service learning. According to the survey responses, little difference exists in instructional practices between public and private institutions, across high, medium, and low selectivity institutions, and across institutions of various sizes.

"Notably, the survey indicated that any activity involving students entering the work place, for internships, work shadowing, paid or volunteer employment, is as rare in these career planning courses as educational travel or service learning."

All of the career planning courses reported on in this survey have been offered for more than one year, with most reported to have existed for between six and 10 years. Respondents noted that students and to a lesser extent faculty are involved in evaluating these courses, nearly all which are subjected to such a process. On the other hand, these courses are generally reported not to be part of institution-wide assessment. According to these survey respondents, neither of the courses from highly selective institutions are involved in an institution-wide assessment process, five of 20 courses from medium selectivity institutions are part of this kind of assessment, and one of the four courses from low selectivity institutions is involved. None of the three courses reported on in this survey from the largest sized institutions participate in such assessment. Overall, only 23% of respondents indicated that career planning courses are part of comprehensive assessment.

"Other" Courses

Forty respondents described courses under the "other" category. These courses were described by three respondents as intending "to acquaint students with basic ethical frameworks for making decisions," "to promote understanding of the relationship between technical work and society," and "to foster integration and synthesis around a complex problem or intellectual issue." Twenty nine of these surveys were returned from respondents at private institutions, 11 from respondents at public institutions, 9, 29, and 3 from respondents at high, medium, and low selectivity institutions, respectively, and 9, 20, 1, and 10, respectively, from respondents at institutions enrolling the following number of students: under 1,000, 1,001 to 5,000, 5,001 to 10,000 and more than 10,000 students.

Despite their classification as different from all other courses described in the survey, these courses, as reported, share many of the same number one goals with the other course types, beginning with fostering integration and synthesis within the academic major and promoting integration and connections between the academic major and world of work. None of the respondents reported that these courses are intended to address personal adjustment issues or postgraduate education.

Consistent with most of the other 824 courses described in this survey, "other" courses are reportedly not intended to focus on general education, either as a topic in its own right or as it relates to the academic major. Little difference in this regard exists across institution types, selectivity or enrollment levels. According to the responses, little difference also exists across institutions regarding who teaches these "other" courses. They are reported to be taught almost exclusively by faculty. The respondents indicated that these courses are just as likely to be taught in instructional teams as by faculty working alone, setting them apart from many other courses described in the survey. These courses are reportedly not taught by career center professionals, other student affairs professionals, or graduate students. Respondents noted that seven community and workplace professionals are involved in the equivalent number of courses, either as instructors working alone or as members of instructional teams.

More than half of the respondents indicated that these courses are administered by individual academic departments, with a smaller number administered by more than one department or centrally. Three respondents indicated that general education departments administer these courses.

"According to respondents, private institutions are almost twice as likely to hold very small classes than public institutions and institutions of medium selectivity offer larger courses than either the least or most selective institutions."

"Other" course sections are reported to be among the smallest of all of those described in the survey. Forty two percent of respondents indicated that the "other" course sections they were reporting on enroll fewer than nine students, 62% of respondents indicated that "other" course sections enroll fewer than 20 students, and only three of these courses are reported to enroll 40 or more students. According to respondents, private institutions are almost twice as likely to hold very small classes than public institutions. Institutions of medium selectivity offer larger courses than either the least or most selective institutions. Institution size does not appear to make as great a difference in the size of enrollments in these courses as other factors.

This survey suggests that highly selective, small, and private institutions are less likely to grant letter grades for "other" senior seminars and capstone courses, although across institution types granting letter grades is still the prevalent practice. More than 80% of respondents indicated that these courses are assigned letter grades. The larger and less selective the institution, the more likely it is to grant a letter grade rather than to designate these courses pass/fail. Responses indicate that the largest institutions also tend to offer these courses for academic credit more frequently than small institutions although, again, 80 to 100% of respondents indicated that these "other" courses are offered for academic credit. The majority of these courses, according to the respondents, are offered at semester system schools, where they are generally offered for three semester credit hours and are one semester in length.

Only two respondents answered the survey question about the ratio of males to females in elective "other" senior seminars and capstone courses. Both indicated that these elective courses are more heavily subscribed to by women than men. Respondents indicated that "other" courses are the type of courses generally required by the departments offering them, and they have existed on their campuses for up to 15 years. Two private institution courses are reported to have existing for nearly 50 years. Private institution "other" courses in this survey, overall, tend to be older than their public school equivalents, as are courses at smaller and more highly selective institutions. According to the respondents, these courses are taught very much like other department-administered courses reported on in this survey.

"Service learning does appear higher on the list of instructional components of "other" courses than other types of courses described in the survey."

The instructional component that is reported to predominate is the oral presentation, followed by the major project. Portfolio development, the third most frequently reported instructional technique in these courses, differentiates them from most discipline- and department-based courses except those in departments offering pre-professional degrees. According to the respondents, just under one-third of these "other" courses also employ internships, which sets them apart from all other course types. As noted in Chapter 1, several "other" courses were described narratively by respondents as internship opportunities.

Respondents listed a variety of other approaches to teaching these courses including product development, use of written case studies, research presentations, performances, and résumé' writing. The respondents indicated that instructors of these courses are least likely to ask their students to conduct work shadowing, that they are not likely to provide leadership training, that they do not generally involve alumni in the courses, that they do not require a thesis from their students, and that they do not have the students use the career center. Service learning appears higher on the list of instructional components of "other" courses than other types of courses described in the survey. The selectivity level of institutions appears to be the greatest determinant of instructional component choice, although the number of responses is too small to draw solid conclusions. The strongest correlation between instructional component in these "other" courses and selectivity relates to service learning. Half of the eight "other" courses at highly selective institutions are reported to employ this instructional technique, whereas only four of the 29 courses at medium selectivity institutions use this approach.

According to the respondents, these "other" courses are evaluated at the same high level as discipline- and department-based courses and are evaluated most often by the involved students and faculty. Little difference exists across institution type. A higher percentage of these courses are involved in comprehensive assessment than other courses, with nearly 60% of respondents who indicated that these courses are involved in such an effort.

Chapter 6

Summary of Analysis and Conclusions

With all that America's institutions of higher education must attend to, focusing on students months away from leaving, perhaps for good, seems more luxury than necessity. After all, as noted in Chapter 1, these students have demonstrated dogged perseverance and a capacity to succeed in a system that jettisons many of their peers. Why train limited energy and resources on them?

For reasons of institutional viability and profound obligation to all students, paying attention to seniors is more than a perfunctory or ceremonial responsibility. By the time these students arrive at their senior year, their expectations are high and their transitional needs acute. They are primed for a valedictory experience, and if, as Gardner and Van der Veer (1998) suggest, this experience is rich and rewarding, graduating seniors may become an institution's greatest supporters. Conversely, these students on the cusp of major life change may feel a sense of disappointment and loss if their experience is managed badly. The senior year is an institution's last chance to provide its students with a quality academic experience and the final opportunity to impart to them the importance of contributing their efforts and resources after graduation to their soon-to-be alma mater (Gardner & Van der Veer, 1998). It is, finally, the most appropriate moment to nurture a practice of reflection and self-evaluation. For multiple reasons, the statement, "it all comes down to this . . . " should be crafted by an institution with care.

Summary of Analysis

The intent of this monograph has been to display and analyze data from the First National Survey of Senior Seminars and Capstone Courses conducted in 1999 through the National Resource Center for The First-Year Experience and Students in Transition. The survey reported here represents the most comprehensive review of college- and university-level senior seminars and capstone courses conducted to date.

The preceding four chapters presented data on 864 courses reported from 707 American colleges and universities including discipline- and department-based, interdisciplinary, transition, career planning, and "other" courses. Chi-square analyses were performed to determine the significance of differences across three key variables: institution type, institution enrollment level, and institution selectivity. Eleven components of the five course types were analyzed including primary course goals, instructional responsibility, maximum section size, amount and type of academic credit and grading practices, institutional unit administering the course, instructional components, populations required to take the course, length of existence of the course at the institution, and evaluation and assessment practices.

Major Findings

Results of this survey suggest that the majority of senior seminars and capstone courses are intended to culminate learning within the major. As reported by these survey respondents, only in interdisciplinary courses are issues related to general education a high priority. Even then, a focus on these issues was generally reported to be of equal, not greater, importance to career and academic major-related topics. For every other course type, respondents reported that revisiting general education is not typically an issue of priority to be addressed in senior seminars and capstone courses. In the career planning and transition courses represented in this survey, general education rarely predominates.

Instructors of these courses are generally reported to be academic faculty members working alone. In some instances, such as nursing, education, and interdisciplinary courses, respondents indicated that faculty members are nearly as likely to instruct these courses in teams as they are to work alone. Across most courses, graduate students and student affairs professionals outside career centers were reported to be least likely to be asked to teach, while community leaders are occasionally asked to serve on instructional teams. Sections of these senior seminars and capstone courses were generally reported to enroll fewer than 30 students. Responses indicate that sections of "other" courses are particularly small, and sections of courses of all types at private institutions, small institutions, and highly selective institutions are smaller than those at public and larger institutions, and smaller than those at institutions of either medium or low selectivity levels.

In the aggregate, these courses were reported most often to be treated as either major or core requirements, although some interdisciplinary courses also are reported to fulfill general education requirements. Most of these courses are reported to be at least one academic term long and most require a major project or oral presentation. Requiring a thesis was reported to occur most often in courses at smaller and private institutions and institutions of higher selectivity levels. According to this survey, courses at public institutions are more apt than those at private institutions to require final examinations and group projects. Development of portfolios appeared most often among the pre-professional majors, humanities courses, and career planning courses. Preparation for graduate school, service learning, educational travel, and on-the-job training were reported to be least important across most courses.

This survey indicates that most senior seminars and capstone courses are evaluated by the students and faculty members who participate in them, and most of these courses, across all course types, are administered through individual academic departments. Fewer than half of the senior seminars and capstone courses reported on in this survey are folded into comprehensive assessment efforts.

Discussion

In 1991, the National Advisory Committee of the then Association of American Colleges (now Association of American Colleges & Universities) published *The Challenge of Connecting Learning* in which it proposed a framework for building a shared understanding of liberal learning within the academic major. The committee's report, extending from the efforts of learned societies across the arts and sciences, suggested that to "facilitate students' integration of their work, major programs should encourage such devices as reflective capstone seminars or intellectual autobiographies in which students interpret the meaning and significance of their learning to date" (Schneider, 1993, p. 62). The committee recommended that, at a minimum, "curricular space should be allotted for faculty-student discussion of this integrating activity"

(Association of American Colleges, 1991, p. 11). The results of this First National Survey of Senior Seminars and Capstone Courses indicate that a high percentage of American institutions are creating such spaces in senior seminars and capstone courses. Moreover, by the amount and type of credit these courses are allotted and by their designation as requirements for graduation, it appears that departments are serious about the role these courses play in their degree programs. The predominant course goal, to foster integration and synthesis within the academic major, clearly reflects the type of learning within the major advocated in the AAC document.

However, the task of the academic major laid out in *The Challenge of Connecting Learning* extends beyond providing opportunities for students to reflect on learning in the discipline to creating opportunities for students to gain critical perspective and connect learning across disciplines. As Schneider (1993) notes, the committee report was clear that the "major is not an end in itself...nor is it best envisioned as a mini-preview of graduate school. For the most part, faculty should recognize that students 'join the community of the major briefly; ultimately, they must disengage and leave' (Association of American Colleges, 1991, p. 12)" (p. 63). The function of the major is to offer opportunities to look within and to look without, to other disciplines and to the world outside of the institution. As Schneider indicates, "The college education as liberal learning must challenge the inherent limitations, the inescapable parochialism of any specific community... " (1993, p. 63).

The survey reported here suggests that undergraduates in most senior seminars and capstone courses are engaged in reflection inside the major and are preparing for the world of work. The evidence is weak that in senior seminars and capstone courses undergraduates are primarily engaged in reflection on learning in the general education curriculum or in learning that links general education to the major. An assumption underlying wording used in the survey instrument was that general education, as a subject in its own right or as it relates to the academic major, would play a noticeable role in these courses. As noted in Chapter 1, senior capstone courses had previously been described as a major vehicle for bringing coherence to the entire curriculum. Results of this survey indicate that general education, alone or in connection with the academic major, predominates only in some interdisciplinary courses. While the prevalence of academic disciplines in contemporary American higher education, briefly discussed below, is generally not disputed, the anecdotal evidence presented at the beginning of this monograph would have predicted a less subordinate position for general education.

Other evidence from this survey corroborates the single disciplinary focus of most senior seminars and capstone courses. As noted at the beginning of this chapter, the majority of courses represented, including many interdisciplinary courses, are taught by one faculty member and administered by a single academic department. They are evaluated by students and the individual faculty members involved, and occasionally by the administering department. They are most often not involved in comprehensive assessment.

Two factors may help explain the inward focus of senior seminars and capstone courses, beginning with the primacy of the academic discipline in the life of the institution. At the mid-point of the 19th century, American colleges and universities shifted away from their roles as providers of a uniform liberal education for all students to divisions by disciplines and the offering of academic majors (Rudolph, 1977). Along with separate disciplines came divisions along academic and non-academic lines. With few exceptions, academic departments continue to offer students courses in major fields of study after the students have successfully completed a set of common first and second-year requirements most often known as the general education curriculum (Simpson & Frost, 1993). Faculty housed in the academic departments continue today to design individual courses, with responsibility for course creation divided differently at different types of institutions. At medium and small-sized institutions, the president and academic vice president are key players, while at larger institutions, faculty from colleges, schools, and academic departments within the university are responsible for curriculum design (Simpson & Frost, 1993). Although there is some evidence that the lines between the disciplines are blurring (Schneider, 1993), this survey suggests that these disciplinary divisions persist across most institution types.

A second explanation for the disciplinary focus of these courses, arising from the first, is a general agreement between faculty and students that courses will be treated as stand-alone experiences. Because contemporary American higher education, with its emphasis in the majors, does not guarantee a uniformity of undergraduate experiences, it cannot easily support efforts of faculty at any level to synthesize learning beyond, at the most, a handful of courses. For this reason, Alfred North Whitehead's charge to foster reflection "[by] utilizing an idea, I mean relating it to the stream, compounded of sense perceptions, feelings, hopes, desires and of mental activities adjusting thought to thought, which forms our life" (1949, p. 13) is most often necessarily confined within the academic specialty.

A second major finding of this study is the co-existence of a reported desire to prepare students for their careers and connect their academic major with the work world alongside an equally strong reported preference for classroom-based activities. Respondents of this survey indicated that instructional practices in these senior seminars and capstone courses tend away from work or community-based activities, including service learning, educational travel, work shadowing, internships, paid employment, or volunteerism. The often expensive and time-consuming nature of such activities may explain a general aversion to their use, as could the uneven outside class time demands on a general student population distinguished today by its diversity more than its uniformity.

There are difficulties, then, in building an experience that truly culminates the college experience and connects it to the world beyond the classroom. Other institutional concerns coming from increased public scrutiny, burgeoning competition from for-profit entities, and the chaos accompanying the explosion of online learning, also currently press upon higher education. And yet, despite, and in some instances because of, these pressures, Schneider and Shoenberg (1998) offer reasons for hope.

> ...for all the sense of dislocation and disruption, there are emerging understandings and practices that can point the academy in a definable and educationally productive direction. For more than a decade, a growing number of colleges and universities have been engaged in an important, but largely unremarked, reexamination of their educational purposes and practices. Much of this rethinking has taken the form of extensive changes in general education programs and graduation requirements.....Assessment mandates also have contributed to reconsideration of the goals and efficacy of baccalaureate learning.

> Taken together, the themes emerging across hundreds of campuses and thousands of separate educational reports express a renewed and contemporary understanding of the kinds of learning students need to negotiate a rapidly transforming world. (p. 2)

This survey indicates that many seniors at America's colleges and universities are beneficiaries of a process to build opportunities in their senior seminars and capstone courses for synthesizing and integrating learning in the major and for linking that learning to the work lives these students may lead after graduation. On the other hand, it appears that many more students will finish their degrees without reexamining in these courses the learning they did before declaring their majors nor will they use their time in these courses to practice the ideas and skills they have learned out in the workplace or community. With regard to these courses, there is much to give us hope and much to give us pause.

Recommendations for Future Research

This study raises more questions than it answers. First, it tells us nothing about activities outside these single courses that certainly exist to augment learning in the classroom. For example, other settings may be designed to allow seniors to reflect on their learning and other experiences in college. As Kusnic and Finley (1993) note, self-evaluation is being engaged in by undergraduates on many campuses, often as part of what are called "student life" activities. Likewise, formal, comprehensive assessments may also be conducted elsewhere. And the fact that many senior seminars and capstone courses do not provide opportunities for experiences outside the classroom, including volunteer and paid work, does not mean these soon-to-be graduates are not engaged in these activities. Because the senior year, and all college years, are more than a sum of courses, it is appropriate to use qualitative and quantitative approaches to understanding the rich tapestry of the entire senior experience. Similarly, the goals specified in this survey for senior seminars and capstone courses may well be addressed in other courses or across several courses. Cuseo (1998) built the goal taxonomy (used to create this survey instrument) from his research on institutional practices across the entire Senior Year Experience, not just those in single courses. And, as the American Association for Higher Education's Steve Ehrmann (personal communication, October 4, 2000) pointed out recently, it would be difficult to imagine that a single course could successfully cap an entire college experience.

With further regard to goals of these courses, this survey makes a contribution to our understanding of senior seminars and capstone courses but does not go far enough. For example, general education is not synonymous with liberal learning, so we still do not know how many of these courses integrate the precepts of interdisciplinarity and liberal education. What we know from this survey is whether or not respondents indicated that general education, as a topic alone or as it relates to the academic major, predominates in these 864 courses. Furthermore, the use of the term "general education" is somewhat problematic given that it carries no generic meaning across institutions (Osterlind, 1997). Another study using broader, commonly understood descriptors for liberal education (if they could be found) might achieve a different result. Also related to course goals, the interest in this study was on the analysis of primary goals of these courses. A second study, using weighted responses, would look deeper into secondary goals and beyond.

Future researchers may also wish to take a more normative approach to understanding what happens inside these courses. The instructional components respondents were allowed to select from were all student-driven projects and activities. There is a high likelihood that these courses also include faculty-driven pedagogical approaches, including lectures. Another study could ask respondents to describe what weight is given to various instructional components or how much of the course time is spent on various activities, both student- and faculty-driven. Qualitative classroom research including such techniques as micro-ethnography or task analysis would be appropriate here. Furthermore, as the research reported in Hativa and Marincovich (1995) reveals, there are differences in the goals and means of teaching and learning across the disciplines. Future research would compare and contrast the lessons of that research with those of the study reported here.

And finally, much could also be learned from a comparison of first-year seminars and senior seminars and capstone courses. Since the late 1980s, the National Resource Center has conducted national surveys on practices in first-year seminars and by fall of 2000 was preparing to analyze data from the 2000 survey. A cursory examination of practices at the first year and senior year reveals striking differences between the two. A valuable study would offer a careful comparative analysis of these cornerstone and capstone courses.

References

Association of American Colleges. (1991). *Liberal learning and the arts and sciences major. Vol. 1: The challenge of connecting learning.* Washington DC: Author.

Cuseo, J. B. (1998). Objectives and benefits of senior year programs. In J. N. Gardner, Gretchen Van der Veer, & Associates, *The senior year experience: Facilitating integration, reflection, closure, and transition* (pp. 21–36). San Francisco: Jossey-Bass.

Gardner, J. N., Van der Veer, G., & Associates (1998). *The senior year experience: Facilitating integration, reflection, closure, and transition.* San Francisco: Jossey-Bass.

Hativa, N., & Marincovich, M. (Eds.). (1995). Disciplinary differences in teaching and learning: Implications for practice. *New Directions for Higher Education, 64.* San Francisco: Jossey-Bass.

Kusnic, E., & Finley, M. L. (1993). Student self-evaluation: An introduction and rationale. In J. MacGregor (Ed.), Student self-evaluation: Fostering reflective learning (pp. 5–14). *New Directions for Higher Education, 56.* San Francisco: Jossey-Bass.

Osterlind, S. J. (1997). *A national review of scholastic achievement in general education: How are we doing and why should we care?* ASHE-ERIC Higher Education Report Volume 25, No. 8. Washington DC: The George Washington University, Graduate School of Education and Human Development.

Rudolph, F. (1977). *Curriculum: A history of the American undergraduate course of study since 1636.* San Francisco: Jossey-Bass.

Schneider, C. G. (1993). Toward a richer vision: The AAC Challenge. In C. G. Schneider, & W. S. Scott (Eds.), Strengthening the college major (pp. 57–69). *New Directions for Higher Education, 84.* San Francisco: Jossey-Bass.

Schneider, C. G., & Shoenberg, R. (1998). Contemporary understandings and liberal education. *The Academy in Transition, 1,* 1–8. Washington DC: Association of American Colleges and Universities. Retrieved October 3, 2000 from the World Wide Web: http://www.aacu-edu.org/Publications/understanding.html

Simpson, R. D., & Frost, S. H. (1993). *Inside college: Undergraduate education for the future.* New York: Insight Press.

Whitehead, A. N. (1949). *The aims of education and other essays.* New York: Mentor Books. (Originally published 1929).

Appendix A

Examples of Courses

The following documents are examples of 1) a Discipline- and Department-based Course, 2) an Interdisciplinary Course, 3) a Transition Course, 4) a Career Planning Course, and 5) a course classified as "Other." These course examples were provided by respondents, but have been modified to maintain confidentiality.

Discipline- and Department-based Course

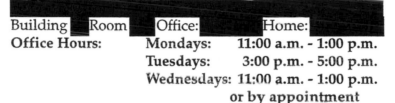

SENIOR SEMINAR — Social Work

SUMMER 1999
INSTRUCTOR:

Building   Room   Office: Home:
Office Hours: Mondays: 11:00 a.m. - 1:00 p.m.
                     Tuesdays: 3:00 p.m. - 5:00 p.m.
                     Wednesdays: 11:00 a.m. - 1:00 p.m.
                                 or by appointment

COURSE DESCRIPTION:
This course is designed to integrate previously learned beginning generalist practice concepts, values, knowledge, attitudes and skills with practice. Corequisite: ██████████

TEXTS:
1. Field Instruction Manual - 2 copies
2. Rothmon, J. (1998). From the front lines: Allyn & Bacon.

COURSE OBJECTIVES: Students are placed in a wide variety of social service settings - public, private and military - which represent many different fields of practice. In this seminar, students are expected to share and reflect on these field education experiences, to discuss problems and issues from the field education experience, and actively participate in discussion and evaluation of practice. Course objectives are to:

* integrate previously learned beginning generalist practice concepts, values, knowledge, attitudes and skills with practice

* develop habits of life long learning through continuing education

* evaluate professional generalist practice skills

* develop a beginning understanding of program evaluation and outcome measures as related to a practice setting

* demonstrate multilevel assessment problem solving and intervention skills

* address diversity, oppression, and discrimination issues in practice

* articulate the integration of theory with practice experience with individuals, families, groups, and community

* analyze social policy as it relates to service provision

Class Participation/Decorum:
Demonstrate professional behavior, attitudes and values.

1. <u>On time</u> attendance is required. All necessary absences must be approved by the faculty. Only illness, emergencies, or similarly serious circumstances will be excused.

    Note: <u>Filling in for sick or vacationing agency staff members is not cause for an excused absence.</u>

2. More than three absences from seminar will result in <u>failure of this course</u>. Two late attendances will equal one absence. The equivalent of three absences will result in the lowering of the final grade by one. (e.g., B to C)

3. Students are expected to be major contributors to each class session. This is a seminar; the expectation is that students will participate in discussion of assigned topics and share agency experiences.

4. Punctuality and professionalism are expected.

5. Students should be prepared to orally present written assignments from the corequisite course in the seminar. <u>These are to be prepared in a professional manner and are to be presented at the assigned time.</u>

6. Confidentiality regarding client information presented in seminar is required.

COURSE ASSIGNMENTS/EXERCISES:

1. Case Presentation:
   Present a psychosocial history/evaluation and ecomap for one client. * <u>This client must differ from the student in ethnicity, culture gender, or sexual preference.</u> Summarize three professional journal articles" addressing the client's ethnicity, culture, gender, sexual preference, or discrimination toward client's groups identity. Use APA style. Name and describe three resources available to the client.

2. Be prepared to discuss field agency experiences related to weekly class topics.

3. Read required texts.

4. Prepare a one to two-page macro project proposal for approval.
   *Please note that "client" may be an individual, a family, a group, or a committee/task force.

**A professional journal article is one which is found in a <u>scholarly</u> journal, is longer than five pages in length, reflects a body of research, and should be current within three years. A case presentation format is attached.

USE OF APA STYLE:
The American Psychological Association's style manual will be followed for all written assignments in the Department of Social Work.

COURSE SCHEDULE: (Schedule may change due to class needs)

Apr	30	Field Orientation Meeting
May	11	Confidentiality issues/videotape and discussion
May	18	Worker Safety Issues * <u>Contract Due</u>
May	25	Agency orientation experiences, agency structure and funding sources. Characteristics of a bureaucracy. Note: Students are expected to contribute to a classroom discussion related to their agency's process of accreditation, quality control and program monitoring.
June	1	Legal Issues * Agency Overview due
June 8		Legal/Ethical Issues * Macro Proposal due * Read entire text
June	15	Ethical Issues
June	22	Generalist Practice Exercises
June	29	Cultural Diversity * Process Recording Due
July	6	Preparation for the world of professional work Speaker: ▮▮▮▮▮▮▮▮▮▮ * Psychosocial due
July	13	Termination Issues
July	20	Case Presentations * Macro Projects Due
July	27	Case Presentations * Submit all revisions

Aug   3   Finals Week

Supervisor Luncheon: Date and preparation to be determined by class. Student participation is mandatory.

GRADES:

Senior Seminar is a competency based course. The objective of the assignments is to help students acquire skills and use knowledge in an agency setting. Work should be submitted on time. Students may revise and resubmit work to produce a highly professional product. Final revisions are due no later than July 27. NOTE: All written assignments must be graded C or higher in order to satisfactorily complete this course.

Three absences will lower the course grade one full letter, for example from B to C. More than three absences, without prior special permission from instructor, will result in failure of the course.

ETHICAL CONDUCT:

Students are expected to demonstrate professional ethical behavior as outlined in the Professional Code of Ethics and the Student's Code of Ethical Conduct. These are in the Field Instruction Manual.

CLASS PARTICIPATION/RESPONSIBILITY FOR LEARNING:

Teachers, through course requirements, presentations and activities, provide opportunities for students to learn. Students have the responsibility to participate, complete requirements and expend the energy necessary to learn information and master skills. Grades are used as a measure of the knowledge and skill level a student is able and/or chooses to demonstrate during a class. Getting grades is not the sole purpose of a course, learning is. Learning requires the learner to stretch, grow and change behavior in some manner. Thus learning will involve some stress and exertion of energy.

PROFESSIONAL CODE OF ETHICS AND STUDENTS' CODE OF ETHICS: The NASW Code of Ethics and the University Honor Code will be followed.

STUDENTS WITH SPECIAL NEEDS: Students with special needs regarding access and completing exams and assignments should inform the professor the first week of class and make arrangements as necessary with Student Services and your professor.

STANDING OF SOCIAL WORK MAJORS: Social Work majors are required to complete all core courses with a grade of C (2.0) or better to be eligible for entry into Field Instruction and graduation.

Interdisciplinary Course

Liberal Arts Senior Seminar: Spring 1999, TTh 11:00–12:20

Course Description

The Senior Seminar provides students with an opportunity to integrate their major area of study with the broader background of their general education program. The course challenges participants to explore their conceptual frameworks or philosophies of life which, in turn, will form the basis for identifying global problems and articulating strategies for confronting them.

Course Goals

1. Students will integrate their general education program and their major area of study, by forging relationships between specialized learning and common human concerns, and by defining the critical assumptions present in their own areas of study.
2. Students will articulate and evaluate their own values, and develop an awareness and understanding of other values systems.
3. Students will understand how conceptual frameworks shape world events and human reactions to these events.
4. Students will investigate their own responsibilities towards the world by analysis of world problems and possible solutions to them, in the realms of personal or family, societal or national, international, and global-environmental concerns.

General Ed. Intended Outcomes, Assessment Tools, Standards of Achievement

1. Oral Communication

Intended Outcome: Students will be able to express themselves orally both by leading and participating in discussion effectively.

Assessment Tool: Discussion will be evaluated each day of class by the seminar leader.

Standards of Achievement: Students will demonstrate they have met the intended outcome to the extent that they:

1. can organize and communicate information in a clear and comprehensible manner;
2. can debate ideas with others in a way which advances discussion of the issue without attacking persons;
3. utilize arguments based on evidence and logic rather than emotion or vague generalities.

Each day students receive a grade for discussion based on this scale:

0   not present
1   physically present but with marginal or non-existent participation
2   adequate oral participation
3   Extremely good participation—very well prepared and involved; may
     introduce outside resource material to the class

(For plenary sessions, students physically present receive a 2, and those who ask questions will receive a 3.)

The student's discussion grade for the course, as evaluated by the instructor, will be calculated and converted to a percentile as follows: $A = 50 + (15 \times P)$ where P is the average daily grade according to the scale above, and A is the percentile grade for participation. Students will also be asked to assess each other's participation at the end of the term, according to a scale to be given at that time.

2. Written Communication
Intended Outcome: Students will be able to effectively communicate their meaning in written work, utilizing conventions of proper writing in the English language.

Assessment Tools: Six position papers and an integrative final paper.

Standards of Achievement: Students will demonstrate that they have met the intended outcome to the extent that they write with a utilization of:
1. proper essay form, e.g., introduction, body, conclusions;
2. proper grammar, spelling, and syntax;
3. clear transitions and paragraphs that follow logically;
4. a writing style that is not vague/choppy but clearly expresses the writer's meaning;
5. comprehensible language rather than verbose jargon;
6. the development of a thesis through evidence, argument, and evaluative conclusions.

Guidelines will be handed out for each written assignment which will specify the questions to be addressed. Grades will be based on how well the student addresses the assigned questions, and the mechanics of writing which will conform to the standards above. The following rubric will be used for grading papers (the percentiles also correspond to those which will be used to determine grades for the course):

95–100%   A+   The student has met all the standards for the assignment to an extraordinary degree, indicating masterful understanding and creativity.

90–94%   A   The student has met all the standards to an excellent degree, with only a few areas needing improvement.

85–89%   B+   The student has met almost all of the standards to an excellent degree, with a few needing extra attention.

80–84%   B   The student has met most of the standards quite well, with some requiring more work to be adequately met.

75–79%   C+   The student has met some of the standards fairly well, but others require considerably more work to be adequately met.

70–74%   C   The student has met some of the standards adequately, but others need significant work to be adequately met.

65–69%   D+   The student has met few if any of the standards adequately, and needs to do some work to meet any of them adequately.

60–64%   D   The student has met few if any of the standards adequately, and needs to do significant work to meet any of them adequately.

0–59%   F   The student has met none of the standards adequately.

The papers will also be used as assessment tools in evaluating how well the student has met the following General Education Objectives.

3. Critical Thinking
Intended Outcome: The student will be able to analyze and interpret different positions on moral and societal issues.

Standards of Achievement: Students will demonstrate they have met the intended outcome to the extent that they can:
1. reproduce the arguments of others clearly and cogently;
2. decide about the validity of arguments based on clear reasons;
3. defend their own viewpoint with logical arguments.

4. Understanding Faith and Ethics

Intended Outcome: Students will be able to form a set of values to assist them in making moral choices throughout their lives.

Standards of Achievement: Students will demonstrate they have met the intended outcome to the extent that they:
1. can define their values and how they make moral decisions;
2. can explain the bases for their values.

5. Historical Appreciation and Understanding

Intended Outcome: Students will understand the historical component of contemporary issues.

Standards of Achievement: Students will demonstrate they have met the intended outcome to the extent that they can:
1. describe the history behind modern political or social situations;
2. analyze possible historical causes and contributing factors.

6. Understanding the Scientific Method and the Implications of Science

Intended Outcome: Students will understand the nature of scientific research and conclusions, and the effect of science on the world.

Standards of Achievement: Students will demonstrate they have met the intended outcome to the extent that they can:
1. describe scientific conclusions and research accurately and clearly;
2. explain the relation of these to global issues and concerns.

7. Multicultural Understanding

Intended Outcome: Students will appreciate the diversity of cultural views.

Standards of Achievement: Students will demonstrate they have met the intended outcome to the extent that they can:
1. compare different cultural views;
2. recognize cultural similarities and differences.

Grade Determination

Each student's grade will be calculated as follows.

Average of six position papers	45%
Final Paper	15%
Attendance	10%
Student peer evaluation of participation	10%
Faculty evaluation of participation	20%

It is expected that all written work will be given to the seminar leader when due; papers will not be accepted via campus mail or e-mail. A penalty of five points will be assessed to papers which are handed in late, until the next class period; after that, a penalty of ten points applies. **Once papers have been read by the seminar leaders and returned to their writers, normally within two class periods, no late papers will be accepted.**

Since the course is conducted as a seminar, students are expected to attend and participate in all regularly scheduled classes. Any absence, whether legitimate or not, will affect a student's participation grade. The attendance portion of the final grade remains at a full 10% for the first two absences, and after that each additional absence lowers the grade for the course one percentage point, regardless of the reason. Seminar leaders rotate among the sections during the semester to maximize variety in discussion and to achieve greater equity in evaluation.

Seminar Leaders

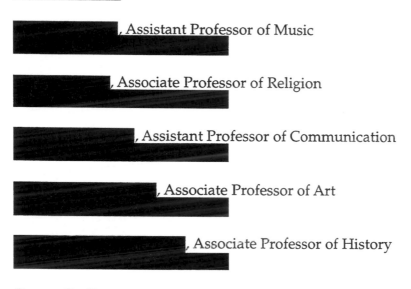

_____, Assistant Professor of Music

_____, Associate Professor of Religion

_____, Assistant Professor of Communication

_____, Associate Professor of Art

_____, Associate Professor of History

Course Outline

1. Constructing a Life Philosophy (2 weeks)
   Bases for moral decision-making
   Developing a philosophy of life
   Students write position paper (3–4 pages)

2. Integrating Specialized Knowledge with Common Human Concerns (2 weeks)
   Discussion of Institutional Mission Statement, Goals, and Objectives
   Examination of Students' Portfolios
   Relation of one's major to General Education and Liberal Arts
   Methods/Values/Goals of those in one's area of study
   Students write position paper (3–4 pages)

3. Issues Facing Modern Society (8 weeks)
   Personal and Family Issues (Family Violence)
   Domestic/National Issues (Censorship)
   International Issues (Human Rights)
   Global/Environmental Issues (Endangered Species)
   Students write position papers on four issues (3–4 pages each)

4. Developing Strategies for Addressing the Above Issues (2 weeks)
   Integration of Course Themes
   Students develop a revised life philosophy in a final paper (6–8 pages)

Texts: The following books are all from the Opposing Viewpoints series from Greenhaven Press. We will be reading portions of each. Assignment sheets for each unit will be given out at the class prior to the beginning of the unit.

Constructing a Life Philosophy, ed. David Bender
Family Violence, ed. A. E. Sadler
Censorship, ed. Byron L. Stay
Human Rights, ed. Mary E. Williams
Endangered Species, ed. Brenda Stalcup

Academic Integrity Statement: Students will be expected to display academic integrity in all their actions in this course. This means that all written work is to be their own and not plagiarized from other students or sources not acknowledged. Plagiarism occurs whenever a person presents words or ideas as his/her own, regardless of whether the student intends to plagiarize or not. Assisting students in committing plagiarism also constitutes a failure to observe academic integrity. The penalty for violation of any of the standards of academic integrity will involve a penalty designated by the instructor which may include failure of the assignment or the course as a whole. All such cases will also be reported to the VP for Academic Affairs of the College.

Liberal Arts Senior Seminar Fall 1998

First Unit Assignments. All readings are from Constructing a Life Philosophy.

Thursday, Jan. 28

Orientation to the Course.
Lecture by ███████ on Values and Morality.

Tuesday, Feb. 2

Come to class having read Ch. 1, selections 1-3 and Ch. 2, selections 1-3. Be prepared to discuss these.
The students in each section will run this discussion, accomplishing the following tasks in accordance with guidelines given that day.
1. Each person should identify her or his own moral decision making "type," from the possibilities given in the handout in Tuesday's lecture. How would you describe your own moral decision making process?
2. Consider the viewpoint of each selection you read, and discuss the following:
a. With what can you agree in this viewpoint? Why?
b. With what do you disagree? Why?
c. Does this viewpoint represent your own philosophy of life?

Thursday, Feb. 4

Come to class having read and be ready to discuss Ch. 4, selections 1-4, plus "Critical Thinking Exercises" on pp. 184 and 203f. The seminar should discuss the following:
1. Can you identify the moral "type" of each of these positions? What are they?
2. With what can you agree in each viewpoint? With what would you disagree?
3. Which is closest to your own moral "type"?

Tuesday, Feb. 9

Come to class having read and be ready to discuss Ch. 4, selections 5 and 6, and Ch. 5, selections 1 and 2. Again consider your views and how they agree or disagree with those of the authors.

Thursday, Feb. 11

Come to class having read and be ready to discuss Ch. 5, sel. 3, 4, 6 and 7.

As a seminar, discuss your moral "types" again; how would you classify yourselves now? What are your central values? Is there consensus in your group, or are there important differences in how you define yourselves and your values?

First position paper assigned; due Feb. 18.

Next unit assignments also given out.

Liberal Arts Senior Seminar: How Will You Live Your Life? Questions to Consider.

What is my goal, my purpose (telos)? What do I value, i.e., what is "the good" in my view? Is it pleasure, happiness, satisfaction, knowledge, power, fame, security, fulfillment, self-actualization, to be a moral person, to excel, to achieve salvation, to serve God, or something else? How do my goals relate to those of others? Do I have responsibilities to family, community, society or nation, the human world, and the world of nature? How are these realms interrelated—what are my duties or goals in relation to them? Can I ignore any of these realms in the pursuit of my own goals, or am I inextricably bound up with these realms so that to ignore them is ultimately self-destructive?

How should I make my moral decisions in life to achieve my goals--on what basis or bases? Are there principles, commandments, guidelines by which I live? Do I follow them consistently, or only when I feel like it?

I.   Teleological Approaches
Acts are justified as moral in regards to the results they intend, i.e., their purpose or intended end (telos): "The ends justify the means." (5.3)
A. Ethical Egoism: My moral choices should intend to increase my own good, my goal (s). This may mean my happiness, knowledge, power, pleasure (hedonism), etc.
(Zindler, 4.3; Ringer, 5.1)
B. Utilitarianism: Moral choices should intend to maximize happiness for the greatest possible number of people. (John Stuart Mill, Jeremy Bentham)
1. Act-Utilitarianism. In a particular situation, one should choose to act in such a way as to maximize happiness for all. There are no set rules prior to situations.
2. Rule-Utilitarianism. One should establish rules prior to situations which will maximize happiness for all, and act according to these in particular situations.
C. Agapism: Moral choices should intend to show "love" (Greek: agape) to the greatest possible number of people.
1. Act-agapism. In a particular situation, one should choose to act in such a way as to maximize love for all. There are no set rules prior to situations. (Fletcher's Christian "situation ethics," 4.1)
2. Rule-agapism. One should establish rules prior to situations which will tend to maximize love for all, and act according to these in particular situations.

II.   Deontological Approaches

Acts are justified as moral in themselves, apart from the consequences they intend or produce. Moral ends never justify immoral means. The justification for an act may be theological (it is God's will or command) or philosophical (it is right or just or kind to act this way, it values persons, etc.)

A. Act-Deontological Theories: One must determine in each situation what is the right thing to do—not by calculating results (as teleologists), but through an "intuition" of what is right. Note: even here, the intuition is based on, e.g., a sense of justice, compassion, fairness, or God's will. One still has reasons for one's decisions, found in basic principles. (Karl Barth's view.)

B. Rule-Deontological Theories: One must establish rules regarding what is right prior to situations, which determine what we ought to do. These rules may be derived from philosophical reasoning or scriptural commands, or both. (Rudnick's Biblical deontology, 4.2)

Liberal Arts Senior Seminar
First Paper Assignment. Due Feb. 18.

What is Your Life-Philosophy?

In 3-4 typed double-spaced pages, reflect on the readings in Constructing a Life Philosophy and our discussions of them. Briefly define your philosophy of life as you understand it at present. There should be two components of this:

1. In the terminology of chapter one, what is the "Map" or "Myth" which you use to structure your life? This involves your world-view (the way in which you view reality) and as such may include your religious beliefs (about God, afterlife, etc.), general philosophical beliefs (about the meaning or purpose of life or the role of humanity in the universe) and your own life goals and values. Is your "map" similar to any of the viewpoints we studied? State as clearly as possible what you believe and why.

2. What is the moral framework within which you make decisions? What bases do you use--are you deontological, teleological, egoistic, agapistic, situational, etc.? What principles or moral rules do you live by? Is your view similar to any of the viewpoints in the text? Reflect on what framework you use, as well as what framework you believe you ought to use.

Your paper will be evaluated on the basis of how well you respond to the questions above; clarity and coherence of argument, and the standards for achievement specified in the syllabus with regards to written communication.

If you quote from a source, give credit, but do not rely excessively on quotation. This is to be your view in your own words. Also, you should realize that this is meant to be a provisional statement of your philosophy, and you will be asked to revise it and present a more extensive statement of it at the end of the semester. One's life philosophy is always developing, and yours will continue to develop long after this course ends; this paper is only meant to be a statement of your views at this time, which you should feel free to change later.

When it is returned to you, please keep your paper, as you will be asked to hand it in again with your final paper at the end of the course.

Liberal Arts Senior Seminar
Second Paper Assignment, Due March 4.

Your Major, Liberal Arts, and Your Life Values

In a 3–4 page typed double-spaced paper, discuss the relationships between your major field of study, liberal arts education, and your life philosophy and values. Integrate your consideration of the following:

1. Your understanding of Liberal Arts Education, as reflected in your view of the institution's mission, goals, and objectives.

      a. Are the values found in these consonant with your own values? Explain.

      b. Does your portfolio indicate that your education has addressed these goals and objectives? In what ways?

2. Your reflections generated by your:

      a. conversation with a faculty member in your field;

      b. conversation with a college graduate on educational goals and values;

      c. reading of a journal article in your field in regards to the values and goals of your career field, its methods, and the relation of your field and its values to liberal arts values—as well as to your own values. Be sure to address a, b, and c as you consider these.

Your reflection paper will be evaluated on the basis of adequate treatment of the assignment, clarity of expression, and the standards for achievement in written communication found in the syllabus.

Liberal Arts Senior Seminar Fourth Paper Assignment, Due April 8.

Censorship

In a 3–4 page typed double-spaced paper, integrate your answers to the following questions related to censorship. Be sure to consider at least three of the following types of "speech" which might be subject to censorship: books in public schools and libraries, flag burning, TV sex and violence, internet speech, pornography, and the types of speech proscribed by campus speech codes.

1. Discuss specific concerns that censorship advocates have about the effects of certain messages.

2. Discuss specific concerns First Amendment proponents have about the effects of censorship.

3. Based on your analysis of the above concerns, what policies do you propose or support regarding these issues?

Your reflection paper will be evaluated on the basis of adequate treatment of the questions, clarity of expression, and the standards of achievement for written communication found in the syllabus.

LIBERAL ARTS SENIOR SEMINAR
SIXTH PAPER ASSIGNMENT DUE THURSDAY, MAY 6

ENDANGERED SPECIES

In 3–4 (or more) pages, discuss in some detail the issues involved in dealing with the "Endangered Species" issue, including, but not limited the following:

1. Using the "attitudes toward nature" described by ███████████, show with some precision and clarity where you stand on the continuum from domination of nature to ecofeminism. Show how your attitude has been shaped by the readings in our text, ███████████ lecture, and most especially by our discussions in Senior Seminar.

    2. Describe how you think the concept of private property relates to the whole question of extinction and the preservation of endangered species. Trace as carefully as you can exactly how complete the "right of private property" is, and what limitations may properly be placed on it by society. What valid arguments do you see that support "private property rights?"

    3. Deal in some significant way with the problem of "endangered peoples." Do you believe that "humans are an endangered species?" Where do you come down on the question of "putting people before nature?"

Your paper will be graded on how well you address the questions above, on the quality of the evidence you present in support of your views, on your clarity of expression, and the standards for achievement in written communication found in the course syllabus.

Liberal Arts Senior Seminar: Final Unit of Course Spring

For the final two weeks of the semester, we have in previous semesters asked students to reflect on the questions for their final papers and make oral presentations on their own answers. This time, largely in response to student input in previous semesters, we are not requiring students to give these oral presentations (though they will still be required to write a final paper addressing these questions). Many students felt that they would rather have had some opportunity in the last two weeks to address topics which have not yet been discussed, whether these be topics of personal, national, international, or global scope. For this reason, we are giving each section the chance to plan how you will spend your final classes, as follows:

May 4   Sections meet to plan the final unit. You may wish to discuss the questions for the final papers (found on the reverse side of this sheet), or ask your faculty leader for clarification of them, but you do not need to do so. What you must do is plan how to spend your time for this class and the two which follow. This might include a discussion of some recent current events not yet addressed by this class, or other issues or topics of relevance to your personal or professional lives. As a group, decide:
          a. What to discuss
          b. What members of the group should read or research for next time
          c. Who needs to report on what topics to the group next time

May 6   Carry out activities planned by the section on May 4. This may include discussion of agreed upon topics, about world events or your personal lives; students might be required to report on their research on such topics, or make presentations. Also, plan for the next class.

May 11   Continue activities planned by the section.

May 13   Final class period for class evaluation, written and oral. Discussion of these last two weeks and the course as a whole. Suggestions to faculty for implementation next year.

You may use small groups or one discussion group as the need arises and as the group decides. Note that your faculty leader will take part to the extent that you encourage him or her to do so; he or she may be an active participant, or simply an observer. In any case, the faculty leader will evaluate the participation of all students not based on the amount of talking they do, but on how responsibly they carry out the task of planning and conducting meaningful discussions on the issues you have chosen.

On the other side, you will find the questions that need to be answered in your final papers. There is no final exam for this course.

The following questions should be answered in your final paper, due to your section leader by Noon, May 19. It should be 6–8 pages, double spaced.

1. What common themes have emerged for you from the consideration of the issues we discussed in this class (family violence, censorship, human rights, endangered species)?

2. What moral responses have you had to each of these issues? Does anything link these together, e.g. certain principles or values which have guided you in making decisions about them?

3. Is there any connection between these moral responses and your initial statement (in your first paper) regarding your values and philosophy of life? Have you actually used those values in addressing these issues? Why or why not? What values have you used?

4. How has the consideration of these issues affected your philosophy of life? Have you modified your framework for moral decision making? If not, would you articulate it any differently? In what ways?

5. What role do the values of the liberal arts philosophy, and those of your career field, play in your life philosophy and values?

6. To the extent possible, outline individual and societal strategies for addressing these or similar issues. What does your moral system require in order for you to leave this world a better place in which to live?

Transition Course

Leadership in Student Development - Senior Transition

The Senior Year Experience - A Transition to the World of Work

Summer Quarter

Course Information:	Class Day:	Tuesday
	Class:	1–4PM
	Class Location:	███████████

Required Text: *Ready for the Real World, First Edition*
William C. Hartel, Stephen W. Schwartz,
Steven D. Blume, & John N. Gardner
Wadsworth Publishing Co., Belmont, CA, 1994.

Additional Requirements: Each student will be required to take the Myers-Briggs Type Indicator (MBTI) and the Strong Interest Inventory (SII). A $15 direct charge to your University Bursar account will automatically be done when you take the MBTI and SII. If you have taken either instrument within the last year, those results will be used.

Instructor Information:
Name: ██████████████
Office: ██████████████
Phone/FAX: ██████████████
Email: ██████████████
Office Hours: **Monday 10 12 noon
**Wednesday 3–5 p.m.

**These hours are tentative and subject to change. Changes will be discussed in class one-week prior, if at all possible. Other times are available by appointment.

Course Description:

The central focus of the course will be on the practical, developmental, and psychological elements experienced during the successful transition from life as an undergraduate student to the life of a citizen/worker. Emphasis will be placed upon integrating academic experiences into postgraduate plans of employment and life outside college. An intensive career planning process will be used to incorporate self-awareness, career exploration, and self-marketing techniques into plans for successful employment and career goals after college. The course will cover a holistic dimension of practical issues that deal with the process of leaving college, including the following: personal, social, vocational, political, civic, financial, and psychological.

Course Goals: After completion of this course, the student should be able to:

1. Prepare for the process of transition during and after their senior year, including examination of individual developmental issues (such as personal, social, vocational, financial, political, civic, spiritual, physical, and psychological) from a developmental perspective.

2. To understand and implement the components of a career development and planning process.

3. Demonstrate improved writing and speaking skills in assignments of both an academic and professional nature.

4. Work as an effective member of a team to analyze, evaluate and decide the best courses of action, when confronted with difficult problems.

5. Organize, monitor team progress, and present their work to their peers for critical review and discussion.

6. Evaluate the practical issues facing graduating seniors through a series of seminars conducted by practicing professionals in areas such as deciding where to live, and work; buy or rent a home, automobile and insurance; alumni involvement and responsibilities; adapting to the first year on the job; traveling for business and pleasure; managing wellness; and how best to adapt to new relationships and lifestyles.

7. Prepare a professional portfolio, resume and cover letter and successfully interview for their career position of choice.

Major Course Requirements:

1. *Active Participation/Attendance (20%):* Each student will be expected to read all assigned readings prior to class, and to be prepared to participate in discussion, in the question/answer/evaluation portions of presentations by fellow students, as well as with guest speakers.

    a. **Class Presentation and Discussion** (5%) - Each student will present a 5-minute summary of an article to the class on a topic related to transitions or career development after college. Handouts for the instructor and each member of the class will be a one-page summary, and a clear copy of the article. An additional 5 minutes will be used to discuss the implications of the article and to answer questions.

    b. **Attendance** (15%) - Due to the fact that this course is highly interactive and a variety of topics are covered, **participation and class attendance are mandatory, and will be assessed daily.** In addition, when guest speakers are invited, these professionals are giving of their time and expertise to visit with the class. For this reason, students are expected to participate by being prepared to ask relevant questions of our guests. All requests for excused absences should be brought to the instructor's attention as early as possible. Students should do all in their power to avoid being late for class. Two late arrivals to class will count as one absence, unless the instructor agrees the tardy arrival was beyond your control. If you arrive late for class, it is your responsibility to inform the instructor at the end of the class to make sure you are recorded as present for class. **For each unexcused absence, your earned final grade will be reduced by a full letter grade.**

2. *Career Planning Process (40%):* In order for you to master the skills necessary for career development and enhancement, this area of work will involve learning and implementing the processes of self-assessment, career exploration, decision-making, and self-marketing, which are all necessary for successful transitions from college to the world of work and for future career changes. This process will require you to complete all of the following activities:

a. Completion and submission of all exercises and handouts regarding career planning and self-assessment.

b. Completion of the MBTI and SII, including participating in a class interpretation session during the class visit to the Career Development Services (CDS) office.

c. Career Analysis Project:

(1) Write an analysis on your primary occupation of interest by researching the occupation using resources in the RBD Library, CDS, the Internet, and direct contact with organization representatives to investigate the specifics of your field of interest; the main responsibilities; needed training; specifics of the working environment; the job outlook; additional sources of information and job leads for the occupation; potential earnings and intangible, personal and professional characteristics of the position. This report should be 2–4 double-spaced pages in length.

(2) Conduct an informational interview with a professional (either in-person or by phone) working directly or indirectly in your field of interest using the procedures and questions outlined in your text on pages 39, 40 and 41. This report should be 1–2 double-spaced pages in length.

(3) Submit a cover letter, a resume, and a 1–2 double-spaced strategic marketing plan that maps out your job search strategy to include resources that will aid you in finding your first professional job. Refer to the Career Development Service's Handbook, pages 16 and 17 to give you a good guide for drafting your paper.

(4) Create a portfolio *table of contents* and plan of action incorporating items (1, 2, & 3) above in an effort to integrate the results of your overall development and activity/work efforts during your college career. What progress have you made? What have your learned? What mistakes have you made? Direct these answers toward the elements of your marketing plan for your number one job target. The table of contents will involve listing "products" such as papers, awards, student organizations, projects, committees, etc. that you have produced or been a member of during your college career, which illustrate your accomplishments and skills related to marketing yourself to employers. The plan of action describes how you will use the portfolio to illustrate your experience, strengths, and talents that make you an ideal candidate for the job you are seeking. Portfolio formats can be chronological or functional. Each student will present their portfolio outline and plan of action to the class.

3. *Team Project (20%):* The class will be divided into teams of 3–4 members whose assignment will be to analyze a city of their choice as a potential site for college graduates to live and work. Project structure should be organized around three themes: strengths, weaknesses, and uniqueness. Information should include analysis of economic, financial, social, climate, and cultural elements, as well as an overview of major employers in the area. Grades will be based on organization, presentation, and depth of information developed. Each member of the group will participate in the presentation, and professional dress, handouts, and visual aids are expected.

4. *Examinations (20%):* There will be an in-class mid-term exam, and final exam given based on assigned readings, class presentations and discussions, handouts, article presentations, and lab seminar discussion. Each exam will be open book and the use of notes and handouts are also encouraged.

Course Policies:

1. Students are expected to attend all classes and to arrive on time. Penalties will be as described in the **Major Course Requirements** section of this syllabus.

2. Late assignments will result in a 10% per-day grade reduction for the assignment.

3. **Disability Statement:** Students who have a documented disability should notify the instructor as soon as possible, but not later than the first two weeks to discuss their needs.

4. **Academic Honesty Statement:** Students and faculty are required to abide by the Student Academic Honesty Code described on page 83 of the ▮▮▮▮▮▮▮▮ and on pages 123, 124, and 125 in greater detail.

5. Incomplete grades and absences beyond the minimum will be considered only for bona fide medical reasons (see ▮▮▮▮▮).

6. Written reports will be submitted to the instructor typed (size 12 font), and double-spaced in either Word or WordPerfect.

▮▮▮▮▮▮▮▮

Grading Policy: The final grade will be determined by evaluating your performance against the following point system:

1. *Attendance/Active Participation*   *100 Points*
2. *Career Planning Project*   *200 Points*
3. *Team Project*   *100 Points*
4. *Mid-Term Examination*   *50 Points*
    Final Examination   *50 Points*

Your total number of earned points will then be compared to the following scale to determine your final grade:

A = 450 - 500 (90 - 100%)
B = 400 - 449 (80 - 89%)
C = 350 - 399 (70 - 79%)
D = 300 - 349 (60 - 69%)
F = 299 or less (59% or less)

Leadership in Student Development - Senior Transition

The Senior Year Experience - A Transition to the World of Work

Summer Quarter

<u>**Course Syllabus:**</u>

Class # 1–   *Course Introduction, the MBTI and the SII.*

<u>**Assigned Reading:**</u> Chapters 1–2

Class # 2 –   *Life and Career Development Processes*

<u>**Activity:**</u> MBTI and SII Interpretation & Tour of Career Development Services (CDS)

<u>**Assigned Reading:**</u> Chapter 3

Class # 3–   *The Job Search Process - Developing A Portfolio*

<u>**Guest Speaker & Activity:**</u> Using the ████ Library in Your Job Search & Research on Companies and Cities

████████, Social Sciences Department ████████ Library ████ University

<u>**Assignment Due:**</u> 1 page self-assessment exercise
<u>Assigned Readings:</u>   Chapters 4 & 17
                           Harvard Business Case

Class # 4 –   *Your First Year On the Job*

<u>**Guest Speaker:**</u> Selecting Location to Live & How to Get Involved

████████, Executive Director ████ Chamber of Commerce

<u>**Assignment Due:**</u> Career Analysis Project (1) Due
<u>**Assigned Readings:**</u> Chapters 9 & 14
                         Plan A Budget Exercise

Class # 5 –   *Financial Planning & Mid-Term Exam*

<u>**Guest Speaker:**</u> Financial Planning - Savings, & Insurance

██

<u>**Assignment Due:**</u> Career Analysis Project (2) Due
<u>**Assigned Reading:**</u> Chapters 11, 12, & 15

Class # 6 –

Relationships & Lifestyle Choices

Guest Speaker: Adapting to Relationships & Personal Change

████████████████, Staff Psychologist Student Counseling Services

Assignment Due: Career Analysis Project (3) Due
Assigned Reading: Chapters 5, 12, & 18

Class # 7 –

Diversity in the Workplace

Guest Speaker: Buy versus Lease (Automobiles)
████████████, Sales Manager, ████████████████

Assignment Due: Career Analysis Project (4) Due
Assigned Reading: Chapters 21 & 22

Class # 8 –

Portfolio Presentations

Guest Speaker: What are Alumni?

████████████, Director of Marketing
████ Alumni Association

Assignment Due: Team Project Outline Due

Class # 9 –

Group Presentations
Activity: Interviewing Practice and Techniques
Comment: Remember to dress professionally!

Class # 10 –

Course Wrap-up and Final Exam

Comment: Class will be held from 5 p.m. to 7:30 p.m.

Career Planning Course

COLLEGE OF HEALTH SCIENCES
PHYSICAL THERAPIST ASSISTANT PROGRAM

I. **COURSE TITLE:**   Interdisciplinary Professional Seminar

II. **COURSE NUMBER:**   ██████████████

III. **CREDIT HOURS:**   2

IV. **CONTACT HOURS:** 30 lecture (1:1)

V. **COURSE DESCRIPTION:**

> This course is discussion/lecture designed to provide the student with current information concerning issues in the field of rehabilitation and to provide preparation for the licensing procedure. The student also will prepare for job seeking by doing cover letters, resumes and mock job interviews. A prerequisite for the course is ████████████.

VI. **COURSE OBJECTIVES:**

At the completion of this course, the student will:

A. Demonstrate an understanding of the procedure to obtain licensure as a PTA in the desired state of practice.

B. Demonstrate an understanding of the process involved in seeking employment as a PTA.

C. Demonstrate an understanding of the role of adjunctive therapies in the treatment of physical therapy clients.

D. Demonstrate an understanding of the role of the physical therapist and physical therapist assistant in different treatment settings.

E. Identify current issues in physical therapy and share this information with classmates.

F. Demonstrate basic skill in summarizing professional journal articles.

G. Demonstrate job readiness skills.

VII. **LECTURE/LABORATORY SCHEDULE:**

The lecture schedule for this class is as noted in the printed College schedule. Any changes will be noted by the course instructor.

VIII. COURSE POLICIES AND EXPECTATIONS:

Policies as outlined in the student handbook are applicable to this course. In addition the following policies will be enforced:

A. For each day an assignment is late, one full grade will be deducted;

B. For each incidence of lateness (> 7 minutes from the beginning of scheduled class time), seven (7) points will be deducted from your total score;

C. If greater than 4 incidents of being late occur, your final course grade will be lowered by one full grade;

D. For each unexcused absence, 15 points will be deducted from your total score;

E. If greater than 2 unexcused absences occur your grade will be lowered by one full grade.

IX. METHOD OF EVALUATION:

A total of 350 points is available in this course.

324 - 350	A
296 - 323	B
268 - 295	C
240 - 267	D
Below 240	F

Cover Letter	50
Resume	80
Oral Presentation	100
Article Review	70
Job Search	50
	350

A "C" or better must be attained in this course in order to meet the requirements for graduation from this program.

X.   REQUIRED TEXTBOOKS:

No required texts. Materials will be distributed in class or available in the library.

"Other" Course

Author's Note: 450 is the senior course.

PERSONAL DEVELOPMENT PORTFOLIO

The Personal Development Portfolio Program is a unique program designed by the College to enable the development of graduates as whole persons. PDP challenges each student to develop academic skills for success through the selection of courses, majors, organizations, and projects. Advisors assist students to set goals for a lifetime, document growth, and develop specific practical skills which will insure futures in graduate schools and careers. Personal development should be demonstrated in the eight dimensions of Academics, Citizenship, Cultural Awareness, Ethical Development, Esthetics, Leadership, Social Skills, and Wellness.

PDP 150 is a one-hour **course.** Activities largely involve small group work in a classroom setting. All sections will use the same syllabus and all students will complete the same requirements for a grade. Both faculty and students will, however, have *considerable flexibility* in the selection of specific classroom activities, discussion topics, and in the selection of activities which meet out-of-class requirements.

PDP 250, 350, and 450 are **advising programs** which include specific requirements and therefore grant academic credit of one hour each. Students will be assigned to faculty members in their major department through the departmental chairperson in consultation with the registrar. Ideally this advisor will remain the student's advisor/mentor for the remainder of the student's tenure at ▆▆▆▆▆ College, thus insuring a continuity of advising. Departments and faculty will interact with student advisees to insure that all academic requirements for graduation are met and to facilitate their students' development in the areas/dimensions introduced in PDP 150.

The personal essay including personal goals is written and revised annually. A minimum of ten hours of service learning is expected each year, and the attendance at convocations, lyceums, and lectures is strongly encouraged and integrated with the PDP program. Departments also plan functions specifically for their majors as well as others. Satisfactory completion of PDP 450 is required for graduation of all students.

PDP 150. Personal Development Portfolio (1FS)
The goals of this course are to introduce students to the mission of ▆▆▆▆▆ College, to improve the transition to college, and aid personal development in such areas as academic achievement, ethical and cultural awareness, health issues, citizenship, and leadership. Other goals such as choosing a major, developing good academic skills (time management, study skills, goal setting), and becoming active in campus affairs are also stressed. The first written personal essay is required.

PDP 250. Personal Development Portfolio (1FS) The goal of this year is to establish the relationship of the student with an advisor/mentor in the field of major study. With personal interviews the advisor aids the student to set goals for the future and for the year. Becoming involved in organizations, considering positions of leadership, and completing at least one activity in each of the personal dimensions is encouraged.

PDP 350. Personal Development Portfolio (1FS) This level encourages a student to accomplish activities in each of the personal dimensions, some of which demonstrate leadership development. A relationship should be established with the Career Counseling Center. Students may be encouraged to begin planning internships and practical experiences. Practice of interviewing skills and the first written resume may be required.

PDP 450. Personal Development Portfolio (1FS) PDP 450 is required for graduation of all students. The contents of a student's portfolio are completed, possibly including personal essay, letters of recommendation, reports of internships and practical experiences, examples of academic research and writing, documentation of service learning, a résumé, and a sample cover letter. During the senior year a student defends his or her individual development in each of the personal dimensions, likely in an oral presentation or interview. Departments determine the method of examination in their specific programs.

Appendix B

First National Survey of Senior Seminars/Capstone Courses
National Resource Center for The First-Year Experience & Students In Transition
University of South Carolina, Columbia, South Carolina 29208

1. Name of institution _____

2. City _____ 3. State _____ 4. Zip Code _____

    Your name_____ Title _____

    Department address _____

    Telephone _____ E-Mail _____

5. What is the approximate undergraduate enrollment at your institution? _____

6. What is the approximate number of students with senior classification at your institution? _____

7. Does your institution or do any of its constituent units offer one or more senior seminar/capstone courses?

          ❐ Yes   ❐ No

If your institution does not currently offer a senior seminar or capstone course, please disregard the
remaining questions and return the survey in the enclosed postage paid envelope.
Thank you for your response.

8. If you responded "Yes" to question #7, please indicate which of the following type(s) best describe(s)
    your senior seminars)/capstone course(s). If possible, attach a current sample syllabus or course description
    with the returned survey.

      ❐   a. Interdisciplinary capstone course

      ❐   b. Discipline- or department-based capstone course

      ❐   c. Career planning course

      ❐   d. Transition course focusing on preparation for work, graduate school, life choice, life skills,
            or life after college

      ❐   e. Other (please describe): _____

If your institution offers more than one type of senior seminar or capstone course, please answer the
remaining questions for one type only. Feel free to copy this instrument as necessary to provide a
survey response for each senior seminar/capstone course offered on your campus.

9. Choose one of the five senior seminar/capstone course types indicated in question #8 and use that type as the basis for answering the remaining questions on this survey. Please mark below the type for which you have chosen to respond.

   I am answering the remaining questions for the following course type:

   ☐ a   ☐ b   ☐ c   ☐ d   ☐ e

10. Our evidence to date indicates that senior seminars/capstone courses are most commonly designed to meet one or more of the following goals. Please NUMBER, in order of importance (1=most important), which goals, if any, apply to your course. **Please NUMBER only those goals which are clearly relevant to the course.**

   _____ a. Promoting the coherence and relevance of general education.

   _____ b. Promoting integration and connections between general education and the academic major.

   _____ c. Fostering integration and synthesis within the academic major.

   _____ d. Promoting integration and connections between the academic major and work world.

   _____ e. Explicitly and intentionally developing important student skills, competencies, and perspectives which are tacitly or incidentally developed in the college curriculum (e.g., leadership skills).

   _____ f. Enhancing awareness of and support for the key personal adjustments encountered by seniors during their transition from college to post-college life.

   _____ g. Improving seniors' career preparation and pre-professional development.

   _____ h. Enhancing seniors' preparation and prospects for postgraduate education.

   _____ i. Promoting effective life planning and decision making with respect to issues that will be encountered in adult life after college.

   _____ j. Other (Please describe): _____

   _____

11. Who teaches the course? Please check all that apply.

   ☐ a. Faculty

   ☐ b. College/university career center professionals

   ☐ c. Other student affairs professionals

   ☐ d. Community/workplace professionals

   ☐ e. Graduate students

   ☐ f. Other (please identify): _____

12. Is the course team taught?   ☐ Yes   ☐ No

13. What is the maximum section size for your senior seminar/capstone course? _____

14. How is the course graded?   □ Pass/Fail   □ Letter grade

15. Do students receive academic credit for the course?   □ Yes   □ No

16. If yes, how many credit hours? _____ *(PLEASE CIRCLE:* quarter / semester / other hours)

17. This credit is treated as a(n):
   □ a. core requirement
   □ b. elective
   □ c. major requirement
   □ d. general education requirement
   □ e. other (please identify): _____

18. If your course is an elective, and if your institution is coeducational, please
   give us an approximate gender ratio for the student enrollment patterns. _____
                                                                            male : female

19. Over what length of time is the senior seminar/capstone course offered? _____ _____
   (example: six weeks, one semester)

20. What campus unit administers the course? _____

21. Does the course include any of the following components? (Check all that apply.)

   □ a. Thesis   □ k. Educational travel
   □ b. Final exam   □ l. Use of career center
   □ c. Major project   □ m. Alumni involvement/networking
   □ d. Portfolio development   □ n. Explicit consideration of graduate school
   □ e. Oral presentation   □ o. Leadership training
   □ f. Group project   □ p. Other culminating project or activity
   □ g. Internship   (please explain): _____
   □ h. Work shadowing   _____
   □ i. Employment   _____
         (remunerative, non-remunerative)   _____
   □ j. Service learning/community service

22. Which students are required to take the course?   ❏ All   ❏ Some   ❏ None

    If some, please specify: _____

23. How many years has the senior seminar/capstone course been in existence at your institution? _____

24. Is the course evaluated by any constituent group (i.e., students, faculty, administrators)?   ❏ Yes   ❏ No

    If yes, briefly describe the evaluation method. _____

_____

25. Is the course tied to comprehensive institutional assessment?   ❏ Yes   ❏ No

    If yes, please describe. _____

_____

Thank you for your response. Please return this survey in the enclosed postage paid envelope.

If you have questions about this survey, please call or write the National Resource Center, 1629 Pendleton Street, Columbia, SC 29208. Phone: 803-777-6029 FAX: 803-777-4699 E-mail: carriew@gwm.sc.edu

Appendix C

Responding Institutions

Discipline- and Department-based Courses

Abilene Christian University	Abilene, TX
Alcorn State University	Alcorn State, MS
Alderson-Broaddus College	Philippi, WV
Allen University	Columbia, SC
Asbury College	Wilmore, KY
Ashland University	Ashland, OH
Augusta State University	Augusta, GA
Augustana College	Rock Island, IL
Averett College	Danville, VA
Baldwin-Wallace College	Berea, OH
Ball State University	Muncie, IN
Barnard College	New York, NY
Baruch College/CUNY	New York, NY
Belmont Abbey College	Belmont, NC
Beloit College	Beloit, WI
Bennett College	Greensboro, NC
Bethany College	Bethany, WV
Bethel College	Saint Paul, MN
Birmingham-Southern College	Birmingham, AL
Blackburn College	Carlinville, IL
Bluefield State College	Bluefield, WV
Boise State University	Boise, ID
Bowdoin College	Brunswick, ME
Bradford College	Haverhall, MA
Brenau University	Gainesville, GA
Brigham Young University	Provo, UT
Brigham Young University-Hawaii	Laie, HI
Brown University	Providence, RI
Bryn Mawr College	Bryn Mawr, PA
Bucknell University	Lewisburg, PA
Buena Vista University	Storm Lake, IA
Buffalo State College-SUNY	Buffalo, NY
California Baptist University	Riverside, CA
California State University	Carson, CA
California State University - Bakersfield	Bakersfield, CA
California State University - Northridge	Northridge, CA
California State University, Stanislaus	Turlock, CA
Canisius College	Buffalo, NY
Capital University	Columbus, OH
Carroll College	Helena, MT
Center for Creative Studies-College of Art & Design	Detroit, MI
Central College	Pella, IA
Central Missouri State University	Warrensburg, MO
Central State University	Wilberforce, OH
Chadron State College	Chadron, NE
Chapman University	Orange, CA
Charleston Southern University	Charleston, SC
Christopher Newport University	Newport News, VA
Cincinnati Bible College & Seminary	Cincinnati, OH
Clarkson University	Potsdam, NY
Clearwater Christian College	Clearwater, FL
Cleary College	Howell, MI
Cleveland State University	Cleveland, OH
Coker College	Hartsville, SC
Colby College	Waterville, ME
Colgate University	Hamilton, NY
College of Health Sciences	Roanoke, VA
College of Saint Elizabeth	Morristown, NJ
College of Staten Island	Staten Island, NY
Columbia College	Columbia, MO
Concord College	Athens, WV
Concordia University	St. Paul, MN
Converse College	Spartanburg, SC
Culver-Stockton College	Canton, MO
Cumberland College	Williamsburg, KY
Dallas Christian College	Dallas, TX
Defiance College	Defiance, OH
Delaware State University	Dover, DE
Delta State University	Cleveland, MS
DePaul University	Chicago, IL
Divine Word College	Epworth, IA
Dominican College	San Rafael, CA
Dominican College of Blauvelt	Orangeburg, NY

Dowling College	Oakdale, NY	Inter American University of	
Drake University	Des Moines, IA	Puerto Rico	San German, PR
Drury College	Springfield, MO	Iona College	New Rochelle, NY
East Carolina University	Greenville, NC	John Carroll University	Cleveland, OH
Eastern Illinois University	Charleston, IL	John Jay College of	
Eastern Oregon University	LeGrande, OR	Criminal Justice	New York, NY
Edinboro University of PA	Edinboro, PA	Johnson C. Smith University	Charlotte, NC
Embry-Riddle		Kansas City Art Institute	Kansas City, MO
Aeronautical University	Daytona Beach, FL	Kansas State University	Manhattan, KS
Emmanuel College	Boston, MA	Keene State College	Keene, NH
Emporia State University	Emporia, KS	Kent State University	Kent, OH
Erskine College	Due West, SC	Kentucky Wesleyan College	Owensboro, KY
Evangel University	Springfield, MO	Kutztown University of PA	Kutztown, PA
Fayetteville State University	Fayetteville, NC	Lakeland College	Sheboygan, WI
Felician College	Lodi, NJ	Lander University	Greenwood, SC
Ferris State University	Big Rapids, MI	LaRoche College	Pittsburg, PA
Fisk University	Nashville, TN	Lees-McRae College	Banner Elk, NC
Fitchburg State College	Fitchburg, MA	LeMoyne College	Syracuse, NY
Flagler College	St. Augustine, FL	Lewis University	Romeoville, IL
Florida Atlantic University	Boca Raton, FL	Lincoln University	Lincoln University, PA
Florida Institute of Technology	Melbourne, FL	Lincoln University	San Francisco, CA
Fontbonne College	St. Louis, MO	Lindsey Wilson College	Columbia, KY
Fordham University	New York, NY	Lock Haven University of PA	Lock Haven, PA
Fort Lewis College	Durango, CO	Lubbock Christian University	Lubbock, TX
Framingham State College	Framingham, MA	Lycoming College	Williamsport, PA
Franciscan University of		Lynn University	Boca Raton, FL
Steubenville	Steubenville, OH	Macalester College	St. Paul, MN
Fresno Pacific University	Fresno, CA	Madonna University	Livonia, MI
Furman University	Greenville, SC	Maharish University of	
Gallaudet University	Washington, DC	Management	Fairfield, IA
Geneva College	Beaver Falls, PA	Marist College	Poughkeepsie, NY
George Fox University	Newberg, OR	Marycrest International	
Georgia Institute of Technology	Atlanta, GA	University	Davenport, IA
Georgia Southern University	Statesboro, GA	Maryland Institute	
Gettysburg College	Gettysburg, PA	College of Art	Baltimore, MD
Goshen College	Goshen, IN	Massachusetts College of Art	Boston, MA
Grand Canyon University	Phoenix, AZ	Mayville State University	Mayville, ND
Grand Valley State University	Allendale, MI	McKendree College	Lebanon, IL
Greensboro College	Greensboro, NC	McNeese State University	Lake Charles, LA
Gustavus Adolphus College	St. Peter, MN	Medaille College	Buffalo, NY
Hampden-Sydney College	Hampden-Sydney, VA	Metropolitan	
Hanover College	Hanover, IN	State University	St. Paul, MN
Hastings College	Hastings, NE	Miami University-Ohio	Oxford, OH
Haverford College	Haverford, PA	Michigan State University	East Lansing, MI
Hawaii Pacific University	Honolulu, HI	Middle Tennessee	
Heidelberg College	Tiffin, OH	State University	Murfreesboro, TN
Hendrix College	Conway, AR	Millsaps College	Jackson, MS
Hesser College	Manchester, NH	Mississippi State University	Starkville, MS
Hiram College	Hiram, OH	Mississippi State University	Mississippi State, MS
Hofstra University	Hemstead, NY	Mississippi State University	Meridian, MS
Howard University	Washington, DC	Missouri Southern State College	Joplin, MO
Huron University	Huron, SD	Missouri Valley College	Marshall, MO
Idaho State University	Pocatello, ID	Montana State University,	
Illinois College	Jacksonville, IL	Bozeman	Bozeman, MT
Immaculata College	Immaculata, PA	Montana State University-	
Indiana State University	Terre Haute, IN	Billings	Billings, MT
Indiana University Northwest	Gary, IN	Montclair State University	Upper Montclair, NJ

Morehead State University	Morehead, KY	Rockford College	Rockford, IL
Mount St. Clare College	Clinton, IA	Rosemont College	Rosemont, PA
Mount Union College	Alliance, OH	Saint Anselm College	Manchester, NH
Multnomah Bible College	Portland, OR	Saint Joseph's College	Renesselaer, IN
Murray State University	Murray, KY	Saint Leo College	Saint Leo, FL
Neumann College	Aston, PA	Saint Mary College	Leavenworth, KS
New Jersey City University	Jersey City, NJ	Saint Mary's College	Notre Dame, IN
New Jersey Institute of		Saint Xavier University	Chicago, IL
Technology	Newark, NJ	Salisbury State University	Salisbury, MD
New Mexico		Salve Regina University	Newport, RI
Highlands University	Las Vegas, NM	Sam Houston State University	Huntsville, TX
New York Institute of		Samford University	Birmingham, AL
Technology	Old Westbury, NY	Samuel Merritt College	Oakland, CA
Niagara University	Niagara University, NY	San Diego State University	San Diego, CA
Nicholls State University	Thibodaux, LA	San Jose State University	San Jose, CA
North Central University	Minneapolis, MN	Shepherd College	Shepherdstown, WV
Northeastern University	Boston, MA	Shippensburg University	Shippensburg, PA
Northern Arizona University	Flagstaff, AZ	Simpson College	Redding, CA
Northern Kentucky		Slippery Rock University	Slippery Rock, PA
University	Highland Heights, KY	South Dakota State University	Brookings, SD
Northland College	Ashland, WI	Southern Adventist University	Collegedale, TN
Northwestern College	St. Paul, MN	Southern Illinois University	Carbondale, IL
Northwestern College	Orange City, IA	Southern Wesleyan University	Central, SC
Northwestern State University	Tahlequah, OK	Southwest Baptist University	Bolivar, MO
Northwestern University	Evanston, IL	Southwest Texas	
Ohio Northern University	Ada, OH	State University	San Marcos, TX
Ohio Valley College	Parkersburg, WV	Southwestern Adventist	
Olivet College	Olivet, MI	University	Keene, TX
Oregon State University	Corvallis, OR	Southwestern University	Georgetown, TX
Our Lady of the		Spelman College	Atlanta, GA
Lake University	San Antonio, TX	Spring Hill College	Mobile, AL
Ozark Christian College	Joplin, MO	St. Joseph's College,	
Pacific University	Forest Grove, OR	Suffolk Campus	Patchogue, NY
Paine College	Augusta, GA	St. Thomas Aquinas College	Sparkill, NY
Paul Quinn College	Dallas, TX	State University of	
Paul Smith's College	Paul Smith, NY	West Georgia	Carrollton, GA
Peirce College	Philadelphia, PA	Sul Ross State University	Alpine, TX
Penn State	University Park, PA	SUNY at Old Westbury	Old Westbury, NY
Penn State Altoona	Altoona, PA	SUNY College at Brockport	Brockport, NY
Penn State University-		SUNY Institute of Technology	Utica, NY
Harrisburg	Middletown, PA	SUNY Potsdam	Potsdam, NY
Penn State,		Tabor College	Hillsboro, KS
Worthington-Scranton	Dunmore, PA	Teikyo Post University	Waterbury, CT
Pfeiffer University	Misenheimer, NC	Tennessee Temple University	Chattanooga, TN
Plattsburgh State University	Plattsburgh, NY	Tennessee Wesleyan College	Athens, TN
Point Park College	Pittsburgh, PA	Texas A&M University	Galveston, TX
Polytechnic University	Brooklyn, NY	Texas Lutheran University	Seguin, TX
Pomona College	Claremont, CA	Texas Tech University	Lubbock, TX
Presbyterian College	Clinton, SC	The Catholic University of	
Radford University	Radford, VA	America	Washington, DC
Randolph-Macon		The Citadel	Charleston, SC
Woman's College	Lynchburg, VA	The College of West Virginia	Beckley, WV
Rhode Island School of Deisgn	Providence, RI	The Cooper Union for the	
Rhodes College	Memphis, TN	Adv. Science & Art	New York City, NY
Ringling School of		Thiel College	Greenville, PA
Art and Design	Sarasota, FL	Towson University	Towson, MD
Rochester College	Rochester Hills, MI	Transylvania University	Lexington, KY

Tri-State University	Angola, IN	University of North Carolina	Chapel Hill, NC
Trinity Baptist College	Jacksonville, FL	University of North Dakota	Grand Forks, ND
Trinity College	Hartford, CT	University of North Florida	Jacksonville, FL
Trinity International University	Deerfield, IL	University of North Texas	Denton, TX
Troy State University	Troy, AL	University of Oklahoma	Norman, OK
Troy State University	Dothan, AL	University of Pennsylvania	Philadelphia, PA
Truman State University	Kirksville, MO	University of Pittsburgh at	
Tuskegee University	Tuskegee Institute, AL	Bradford	Bradford, PA
UNC Asheville	Asheville, NC	University of Portland	Portland, OR
United States Air Force		University of Redlands	Redlands, CA
Academy	Colorado Springs, CO	University of Rio Grande	Rio Grande, OH
United States Military		University of Saint Francis	Fort Wayne, IN
Academy	West Point, NY	University of Scranton	Scranton, PA
University of Alabama at		University of Scranton	Scranton, PA
Birmingham	Birmingham, AL	University of South Carolina,	
University at Buffalo	Buffalo, NY	Aiken	Aiken, SC
University of Alabama	Tuscaloosa, AL	University of South Dakota	Vermillion, SD
University of Alabama	Huntsville, AL	University of South Flordia	Tampa, FL
University of Arkansas	Fayetteville, AR	University of Southern Indiana	Evansville, IN
University of California,		University of	
Irvine	Irvine, CA	Southern Mississippi	Hattiesburg, MS
University of California,		University of St. Francis	Joliet, IL
Los Angeles	Los Angeles, CA	University of Tennessee at	
University of California,		Chattanooga	Chattanooga, TN
Santa Cruz	Santa Cruz, CA	University of Tennessee at	
University of		Martin	Martin, TN
Central Arkansas	Conway, AR	University of Texas at Tyler	Tyler, TX
University of Colorado	Colorado Springs, CO	University of the	
University of Dallas	Irving, TX	Incarnate Word	San Antonio, TX
University of Delaware	Newark, DE	University of the Ozarks	Clarksville, AR
University of Evansville	Evansville, IN	University of Virginia's	
University of Georgia	Athens, GA	College at Wise	Wise, VA
University of Hawaii-		University of Washington	Seattle, WA
West Oahu	Pearl City, HI	University of West Alabama	Livingston, AL
University of Illinois at		University of West Florida	Pensacola, FL
Chicago	Chicago, IL	University of Wisconsin	River Falls, WI
University of Indianapolis	Indianapolis, IN	University of Wisconsin,	
University of Kentucky	Lexington, KY	Parkside	Kenosha, WI
University of Maine	Orono, ME	University of Wisconsin-	
University of Mary	Bismarck, ND	Eau Claire	Eau Claire, WI
University of Maryland	College Park, MD	University of Wisconsin-	
University of Massachusetts	Boston, MA	Green Bay	Green Bay, WI
University of Mississippi	University, MS	University of Wisconsin-	
University of Missouri,		Parkside	Kenosha, WI
Columbia	Columbia, MO	University of Wyoming	Laramie, WY
University of Missouri,		Upper Iowa University	Fayette, IA
Kansas City	Kansas City, MO	Urbana University	Urbana, OH
University of Missouri,		Ursinus College	Collegeville, PA
Rolla	Rolla, MO	Utah State University	Logan, UT
University of Mobile	Mobile, AL	Valdosta State University	Valdosta, GA
University of Montevallo	Montevallo, AL	Vermont Technical College	Rudolph Center, VT
University of Nebraska at		Villa Julie College	Stevenson, MD
Kearney	Kearney, NE	Villanova University	Villanova, PA
University of Nebraska at		Virginia Commonwealth	
Omaha	Omaha, NE	University	Richmond, VA
University of Nevada	Las Vegas, NV	Virginia Intermont College	Bristol, VA
University of New Mexico	Albuquerque, NM	Virginia Military Institute	Lexington, VA

Viterbo College	LaCrosse, WI
Walsh University	North Canton, OH
Warren Wilson College	Asheville, NC
Washington College	Chestertown, MD
Waynesburg College	Waynesburg, PA
Weber State University	Ogden, UT
Wells College	Aurora, NY
West Chester University	West Chester, PA
West Texas A&M University	Canyon, TX
West Virginia University	Morgantown, WV
West Virginia University Institute of Technology	Montgomery, WV
Western Carolina University	Cullowhee, NC
Western Illinois University	Macomb, IL
Western Kentucky University	Bowling Green, KY
Western New England College	Springfield, MA
Western State College of Colorado	Gunnison, CO
Western Washington University	Bellingham, WA
Westminster College	New Wilmington, PA
Widener University	Chester, PA
Wilkes University	Wilkes-Barre, PA
William Woods University	Fulton, MO
Williams College	Williamstown, MA
Winona State University	Winona, MN
Wittenberg University	Springfield, OH
Xavier University	Cincinnati, OH
Yale University	New Haven, CT
York College	York, PA

Interdisciplinary Courses

Adelphi University	Garden City, NY
American International College	Springfield, MA
Art Institute of Southern California	Laguna Beach, CA
Augustana College	Sioux Falls, SD
Avila College	Kansas City, MO
Baker University	Baldwin City, KS
Baylor University	Waco, TX
Bellarmine College	Louisville, KY
Benedictine University	Lisle, IL
Bethel College	North Newton, KS
Binghamton University-SUNY	Binghamton, NY
Bluefield State College	Bluefield, WV
Bluffton College	Bluffton, OH
Bowdoin College	Brunswick, ME
Bowie State University	Bowie, MD
Briar Cliff College	Sioux City, IA
Bridgewater College	Bridgewater, VA
Brigham Young University	Provo, UT
California State University - Hayward	Hayward, CA
Carnegie Mellon University	Pittsburgh, PA

Case Western Reserve University	Cleveland, OH
Clarion University of Pennsylvania	Clarion, PA
Clear Creek Baptist Bible College	Pineville, KY
College of New Rochelle	New Rochelle, NY
College of St. Rose	Albany, NY
Colorado State University	Fort Collins, CO
Culinary Institute of America	Hyde Park, NY
Dallas Christian College	Dallas, TX
Dana College	Blair, NE
East Texas Baptist University	Marshall, TX
Eastern Mennonite University	Harrisonburg, VA
Eckerd College	St. Petersburg, FL
Edgewood College	Madison, WI
Elizabethtown College	Elizabethtown, PA
Elon College	Elon College, NC
Emmanuel College	Franklin Springs, GA
Emory & Henry College	Emory, VA
Felician College	Lodi, NJ
Flagler College	St. Augustine, FL
Franklin Pierce College	Rindge, NH
Freed-Hardeman University	Henderson, TN
Goucher College	Towson, MD
Gustavus Adolphus College	St. Peter, MN
Houston Baptist University	Houston, TX
Howard University	Washington, DC
Huntington College	Huntington, IN
Indiana University of Pennsylvania	Indiana, PA
Iowa State University	Ames, IA
Jamestown College	Jamestown, ND
John Wesley College	High Point, NC
Judson College	Marion, AL
Kansas Wesleyan University	Salina, KS
Lambuth University	Jackson, TN
Lincoln University	Jefferson City, MO
Lynchburg College	Lynchburg, VA
Macon State College	Macon, GA
Manhattan Christian College	Manhattan, KS
Marquette University	Milwaukee, WI
Maryville College	Maryville, TN
Medaille College	Buffalo, NY
Metropolitan State University	St. Paul, MN
Mississippi State University	Starkville, MS
Montreat College	Montreat, NC
Mount Aloysius College	Cresson, PA
Mount Vernon Nazarene College	Mount Vernon, OH
Nazarene Bible College	Colorado Springs, CO
New York Institute of Technology	Central Islip, NY
Nova Southwestern University	Ft. Lauderdale, FL

Oak Hills Christian College	Bemidji, MN	Waldorf College	Forest City, IA
Oakland City University	Oakland City, IN	Warner Pacific College	Portland, OR
Ohio State University	Columbus, OH	Washburn University	Topeka, KS
Oregon State University	Corvallis, OR	Wayne State University	Detroit, MI
Ottawa University	Ottawa, KS	Western Maryland College	Westminster, MD
Piedmont College	Demorest, GA	Wichita State University	Wichita, KS
Point Loma Nazarene University	San Diego, CA	Wofford College	Spartanburg, SC
Portland State University	Portland, OR		
Presentation College	Aberdeen, SD		
Puget Sound Christian College	Edmonds, WA	**Transition Courses**	
Ramapo College of NJ	Mahwah, NJ		
Roanoke College	Salem, VA	Allen College	Waterloo, IA
Roberts Wesleyan College	Rochester, NY	Art Academy of Cincinnati	Cincinnati, OH
Rochester Institute of		Auburn University	Auburn, AL
Technology	Rochester, NY	Barber-Scotia College	Concord, NC
Saint Joseph's College	Rensselaer, IN	Barry University	Miami, FL
Saint Louis Christian College	Flurissant, MO	Brevard College	Brevard, NC
Saint Mary's University	Winona, MN	Campbellsville University	Campbellsville, KY
San Francisco Art Institute	San Francisco, CA	College of Health Sciences	Roanoke, VA
Sierra Nevada College	Incline Village, NV	Daniel Webster College	Nashua, NH
Silver Lake College	Manitowoc, WI	Delaware Valley College	Doylestown, PA
Simon's Rock		Florida State University	Tallahassee, FL
College of Bard	Great Barrington, MA	Franklin College of Indiana	Franklin, IN
Southampton College	Southampton, NY	Holy Family College	Philadelphia, PA
Southeast Missouri		Iowa Wesleyan College	Mt. Pleasant, IA
State University	Cape Girardeau, MO	Judson College	Elgin, IL
Southern Methodist		Kennesaw State University	Kennesaw, GA
University	Dallas, TX	Kentucky State University	Frankfort, KY
Southwest Missouri State		Lakeland College	Sheboygan, WI
University	Springfield, MO	Limestone College	Gaffney, SC
Southwestern College	Winfield, KS	Malone College	Canton, OH
St. Edward's University	Austin, TX	McMurry University	Abilene, TX
St. John's Seminary College	Camarillo, CA	Missouri Southern State	
Texas Tech University	Lubbock, TX	College	Joplin, MO
The Master's College	Santa Clarita, CA	Morningside College	Sioux City, IA
The Richard Stockton		Mount Carmel College of	
College of NJ	Pomona, NJ	Nursing	Columbus, OH
Towson University	Towson, MD	Mount Union College	Alliance, OH
Troy State University,		Ohio Northern University	Ada, OH
Montgomery	Montgomery, AL	Oklahoma State University	Stillwater, OK
University of Alabama	Tuscaloosa, AL	Saint Xavier University	Chicago, IL
University of Bridgeport	Bridgeport, CT	Salisbury State University	Salisbury, MD
University of Florida	Gainesville, FL	Southern Oregon University	Ashland, OR
University of Michigan	Flint, MI	Texas Christian University	Fort Worth, TX
University of Mississippi	UniversityvMS	The Juilliard School	New York, NY
University of Missouri	Kansas City, MO	Towson University	Towson, MD
University of Nevada, Reno	Reno, NV	Tri-State University	Angola, IN
University of New Hampshire	Durham, NH	University of Judaism	Bel Air, CA
University of North Texas	DentonvTX	University of Miami	Coral Gables, FL
University of Pittsburgh at		University of North Texas	Denton, TX
Bradford	Bradford, PA	University of South Carolina	Columbia, SC
University of Puget Sound	Tacoma, WA	University of the Arts	Philadelphia, PA
University of Rio Grande	Rio Grande, OH	University of the	
University of South Carolina,		Incarnate Word	San Antonio, TX
Aiken	Aiken, SC	University of West Alabama	Livingston, AL
University of St. Thomas	St. Paul, MN	Valley City State University	Valley City, ND
University of the Pacific	Stockton, CA	Whitworth College	Spokane, WA

Career Planning Courses

Berry College	Mount Berry, GA
Caldwell College	Caldwell, NJ
Campbell University	Buies Creek, NC
Centenary College	Hackettstown, NJ
College of Health Sciences	Roanoke, VA
Crown College	St. Bonifacius, MN
Emory & Henry College	Emory, VA
Graceland College	Lamoni, IA
Heidelberg College	Tiffin, OH
Henderson State University	Arkadelphia, AR
Lander University	Greenwood, SC
Lasell College	Newton, MA
Limestone College	Gaffney, SC
New England Conservatory of Music	Boston, MA
Northeastern University	Boston, MA
Penn State University	University Park, PA
Presbyterian College	Clinton, SC
Saint Joseph's College	Rensselaer, IN
Slippery Rock University	Slippery Rock, PA
Southeast Missouri State University	Cape Girardeau, MO
St. Thomas University	Miami, FL
Truman State University	Kirksville, MO
UNC Asheville	Asheville, NC
University of West Alabama	Livingston, AL
Western Illinois University	Macomb, IL

"Other" Courses

Bates College	Lewiston, ME
Biola University	Los Angeles , CA
Brigham Young University	Provo, UT
Chapman University	Orange, CA
Clemson University	Clemson, SC
College of St. Benedict & St. John's University	Collegeville, MN
College of the Atlantic	Bar Harbor, ME
Concordia University	River Forest, IL
Eastern Nazarene College	Quincy, MA
George Mason University	Fairfax, VA
Grinnell College	Grinnell, IA
Hartwick College	Oneonta, NY
Harvey Mudd College	Claremont, CA
Keene State College	Keene, NH
Lourdes College	Sylvania, OH
Maryville College	Maryville, TN
Meredith College	Raleigh, NC
Minnesota Bible College	Rochester, MN
Mississippi State University	Starkvillle, MS
Mississippi State University	Mississippi State, MS
Ohio University	Athens, OH
Princeton University	Princeton, NJ

Rochester College	Rochester Hills, MI
Saint Francis College	Loretto, PA
Saint Paul's College	Lawrenceville, VA
Samford University	Birmingham, AL
San Jose State University	San Jose, CA
Slippery Rock University	Slippery Rock, PA
St. John's College	Annapolis, MD
Taylor University	Upland, IN
Towson University	Towson, MD
University of New England	Biddeford, ME
University of North Texas	Denton, TX
University of Scranton	Scranton, PA
Villa Julie College	Stevenson, MD
Wesleyan College	Macon, GA
Western New England College	Springfield, MA
Worcester Polytechnic Institute	Worcester, MA

WITHDRAWN

0 0006 00002986

DATE DUE

ease remember that this is a library book,
and that it belongs only temporarily to each
person who uses it. Be considerate. Do
not write in this, or any, library book.